sociological

perspective

RANDOM HOUSE STUDIES IN SOCIOLOGY

 Consulting Editor: CHARLES H. PAGE, University of Massachusetts

Ely Chinoy / SMITH COLLEGE

sociological
perspective

SECOND EDITION, REVISED

AND ENLARGED

RANDOM HOUSE / NEW YORK

9 8 7 6 5 4

Copyright 1954, © 1967, 1968 by Random House, Inc.

All rights reserved under International and Pan-American Copyright Conventions. Published in New York by Random House, Inc. and simultaneously in Toronto, Canada, by Random House of Canada Limited.

Library of Congress Catalog Card Number: 67–30748

Manufactured in the United States of America by The Colonial Press Inc., Clinton, Mass.

Design by *Diana Hrisinko*

preface

The marked progress of sociology in recent decades has been apparent in the expanding body of reliable empirical findings, the development of refined research methods, and the formulation of sophisticated theoretical schemes. Each of these aspects—empirical, methodological, theoretical—is, of course, linked with and in some measure dependent upon the others. The discipline must move on all fronts if it is to maintain continued advance on any.

The growth of sociology has also been accompanied by increasing specialization. In addition to "theory" and "methodology," there are now many "sociologies"—for example, of religion, politics, the professions, mental health, science, the arts, as well as of such familiar areas of sociological inquiry as the family, social stratification, the city, race relations, and crime and delinquency.

Underlying each of the many fields of specialization, however, and basic to the continuing development of the discipline as a whole is an approach or point of view that derives from a set of concepts generally accepted by sociologists. In order to discover what sociology is, therefore, it is necessary to become familiar with these concepts and the perspective they define. This book is devoted to the expo-

sition of this perspective. It is addressed to students beginning the formal study of sociology, to those wishing to review the concepts basic to sociological inquiry, and to the
general reader seeking an understanding of a point of view
that has increasingly permeated contemporary thought.

The presentation of sociological concepts is based upon
two general ideas about their nature. First, although frequently called "constructs" in order to emphasize their
created character, concepts are not simply the arbitrary products of inquiring and imaginative minds. They emerge from
some kind of observation and experience, even when they
refer, as some do, to purely hypothetical entities or processes.
An attempt has therefore been made to suggest the realities
upon which they are based.

Second, concepts are not true or false but more or less
useful. They focus attention upon specific aspects of reality
that may be relevant to the problems with which we are
concerned. Whether or not concepts are accepted, therefore,
depends upon whether or not they prove helpful in our
inquiries.

That there is substantial agreement among sociologists
as to the concepts basic to their discipline does not mean,
however, that there are no differences and disagreements.
Although competing "schools," each with its distinctive conceptual apparatus, have virtually disappeared, there are still
basic issues to be resolved. One cannot, in brief and simple
compass, explore the persisting—and never-ending—problems of conceptual analysis and clarification. Some statements that are open to debate have therefore been offered
without question or qualification. The student who merely
dips into sociology on this one occasion need not concern
himself with these problems. The student who continues to
work in the field will soon become aware of them.

Because sociology also continues to be characterized by
some terminological disorder, it has been necessary on occasion to make more or less arbitrary decisions on usage.

Whenever possible, an effort has been made to indicate alternative terminologies and conceptual differences. It is to be hoped that the occasional use by sociologists of different labels for the same phenomena will not obscure whatever agreement does exist on the fundamental ideas involved.

It has also been impossible in this brief volume to consider the full range of sociological concepts. Some of long standing have been omitted because contemporary research and theory have shown them to be less useful than they were once thought to be or because the realities to which they referred have changed. Nor has it been possible to include those promising suggestions that have yet to be critically and intensively examined; some of them will eventually prove useful, whereas others will turn out to be unimportant.

Although ostensibly a second edition, this book has in fact been revised several times. An expanded version of the first edition appeared as Part One of my *Society* (Random House, 1961). The present edition constitutes, with minor changes, the further elaboration and revision that make up Part One of the second edition of *Society* (Random House, 1967). Beside seeking to remedy the defects of earlier versions and to take advantage of the continuing process of conceptual clarification that goes on in sociology, this edition expands substantially the discussion of the nature and forms of social organization and of the relations between individual and society.

With each revision my indebtedness has grown: to Professor Charles H. Page, whose continuing counsel has been immeasurably helpful; to those colleagues and students who have freely offered their criticisms and suggestions; and to my wife, whose critical judgment and literary sensibility constitute only part of her contribution.

ELY CHINOY

Northampton, 1968

contents

PREFACE *v*

1 Science and Sociology *3*

Sociology as Science *3*
The Objectivity of Science *8*
Science and Concepts: The Problem of Jargon *14*
The Nature of Concepts *18*
The Uses of Concepts *22*
Science and Theory *27*
The Value of Sociology *33*

2 Society and Culture *39*

Patterned Behavior and Collective Life *39*
Society *42*
Culture *45*
The Components of Culture *49*
The Organization of Culture *60*
Role and Status *61*
Groups, Categories, and Statistical Aggregates *68*
Types of Social Groups *74*
Types of Societies *81*

3   *Diversity and
     Uniformity   90*

The Variety of Social Forms   90
Social Uniformities   94
Biology and Society   97
Race   101
Sex Differences   107
Climate and Geography   110
Conclusion   114

4   *Culture, Society,
     and the Individual   119*

Sociological and Psychological Perspectives   119
The Individual as a Social Product   123
Sociological Explanation and the Individual   126
Agencies of Socialization   129
The Process of Socialization   133
Adult Socialization: Continuities and Discontinuities   141
Social Character and Social Structure   144
Individual Differences   149
Postscript   151

5   *Modes of
     Sociological Analysis   158*

The Sociological "Why?"   158
Functional Analysis   161
Manifest and Latent Functions   167
Functional Analysis: Three Cases   171
Social Change and the "Historical" Approach   177
Diffusion   182
Equilibrium and Change   186
Sociology and History   191
Conclusion   195

INDEX   *201*

sociological

perspective

1

science
and sociology

Sociology as science

Sociology seeks to apply to the study of man and society
the methods of science. It rests upon the assumption common to all the social sciences that the scientific method can
make a significant contribution to our understanding of
man's character, actions, and institutions and to the solution of those practical problems that men face in their collective experience.

    The explicitly scientific approach to the study of social
life emerged in the nineteenth century. The word "sociology" itself was coined by a French philosopher, Auguste
Comte, who offered an elaborate prospectus for the scien-

tific study of society in a series of volumes published
between 1830 and 1842. By the end of the nineteenth century a small array of still significant sociological classics had
been produced. In the United States, where sociology sank
its deepest roots, the American Sociological Society had
been established, the *American Journal of Sociology* had
begun publication, and sociology was being taught in several major universities.

Despite these beginnings, however, sociology is essentially a twentieth-century discipline. Many of its ideas and
most of its reliable data have been accumulated only since
1900. Like other sciences its progress has accelerated as the
number of sociologists and the resources available for research have increased. Resistance to the scientific study of
society has gradually waned (although it has not yet totally
disappeared [1]), but many decades were required before sociology gained full acceptance as a legitimate academic
field. Indeed, it was only in the 1950s and 1960s that some
major universities and colleges (Johns Hopkins in the
United States and Oxford and Cambridge in England, for
example) finally incorporated sociology into their curricula.
When the National Science Foundation was set up in the
United States after World War II to support scientific inquiry, sociology was initially excluded but within a few
years managed to establish its claim to funds for research.
In recent years sociological concepts have gained wide currency among scholars in other fields—history, political science, economics, literary criticism—and among practitioners in law, medicine, education, social work, and business.
Sociological findings and interpretations have elicited widespread interest from nonacademic audiences. And these
trends have been evident not only in the United States and
Europe, where sociology was born, but also in many other
nations in Africa, Asia, and Latin America, whatever their
political or religious character.[2]

Reflection about the nature of man and society, even the

recording of careful observations, is of course neither new nor confined to social scientists. Plato's *Dialogues* contain keen and still accurate comments on men's motives and behavior, as do Machiavelli's *The Prince* and Montesquieu's *The Spirit of Laws*. Where can one find a more perceptive discussion of crime and the criminal than in Dostoyevsky's *Crime and Punishment* or a more suggestive exploration of men's concern with social position than in the novels of Jane Austen?

Sociologists should not ignore these sources of insight and understanding or disregard the plays of Shakespeare, the essays of Montaigne, the work of novelists, playwrights, literary critics, philosophers, and theologians. But social science cannot be satisfied with literary insight or philosophic reflection. The tested and verified conclusions toward which the social scientist strives differ markedly from the speculations of philosophers and theologians, the commentaries of reflective observers of the human scene, and the impressions of creative writers. These observations and interpretations are frequently acute and penetrating, but they are also sometimes wrong, or no more than partially true, and they are usually unsupported by systematic or reliable evidence. Samuel Johnson's comment that "Patriotism is the last refuge of a scoundrel" and his remark that "Almost all absurdity of conduct arises from the imitation of those we cannot resemble" are the shrewd judgments of a wise and witty man; yet not all patriots are scoundrels, nor does striving to be what one is not always lead to absurd conduct. At the risk of losing the bite and impact of such neat aphorisms or the aesthetic appeal of great poetry or a wonderfully wrought novel or short story, the sociologist asks for the evidence, tries to identify the conditions under which specific assertions hold true, and recognizes that all conclusions about human behavior are necessarily tentative, including his own.

What are the prerequisites for the scientific study of man

and society and what are its essential characteristics? The
term *science* has been given many meanings. Historically
it once signified any branch of knowledge or study. In the
Middle Ages the seven "liberal sciences" (also known as the
"liberal arts") were the *Trivium* (grammar, logic, and
rhetoric) and the *Quadrivium* (arithmetic, music, geometry,
and astronomy). In modern times science has come to be
used chiefly in two distinct though related ways. It has been
defined as any body of knowledge based upon reliable observations and organized into a system of general propositions or laws. It has also been taken to mean the methods
by which systematic and accurate knowledge about the
"real" world is acquired, as opposed to the intuition, speculation, and more or less casual, though often penetrating,
observations of literature, philosophy, or theology. Intuition and speculation need not—should not—be excluded
from scientific inquiry, but they must become part of a
process in which insight and hunches are subject to careful,
systematic testing and conclusions rest solely upon the authority of logic and fact.

The propositions that make up any body of scientific
knowledge are generalizations; they refer not to individual
events or entities, but to classes or types of phenomena. The
concern of the botanist is not a particular tree or flower,
that of the chemist not the specific reaction in a test tube.
The physicist is not interested in a single atomic explosion,
nor the sociologist in an isolated action or an individual
family. Science is concerned with the repetitive pattern, the
shared attribute or characteristic, those things that events
or elements or trees or persons have in common. All science
rests upon the assumption, so clearly explored and delineated by Alfred North Whitehead, that there is an
"order of nature" which man can discover.[3] Indeed, were
there no such assumption, were there no such order (although here we are making a philosophical assumption),
there could be no science. The introduction of this assump-

tion into the study of man and society was essential for the development of social science.

Science, both as knowledge and as method, incorporates two essential elements—the rational and empirical. As substantive knowledge, science is made up of logically related propositions that must also be supported by empirical evidence. As method, it emphasizes reliable and objective observation and logical analysis. Neither of these elements alone constitutes science. Were any internally consistent logical system to be considered a science, then John Calvin's *Institutes of the Christian Religion* and St. Thomas Aquinas' *Summa Theologica* might claim scientific standing. Alternatively, were any organized body of facts and observations to be described as science, then, as Ralph Ross has pointed out, cookbooks, Sears Roebuck catalogues, and telephone directories would also have to be included.[4]

Scientific generalizations must be subjected, directly or indirectly, to empirical tests. Much of the recorded "social thought" of the past contains theories that seek to incorporate the available knowledge concerning man and society into logical schemes. But no matter how logical or reasonable the generalizations that these theories contain, they have no scientific standing unless they are confirmed by reliable evidence. Frequently they are supported only by isolated examples and casual observation.

Facts alone, however, cannot speak for themselves. Only when they are related to one another, or to general ideas, can they be incorporated into a body of scientific knowledge. The fact that an electric bulb gives off light gains scientific relevance only when linked with other facts concerning both electricity and the filament in the bulb. That the number and proportion of college students in the United States have increased markedly in recent years gains sociological meaning only when this growth is related to the state of the economy, the values of the society, and to other features of contemporary American life.

The objectivity of science

The chief characteristic of both scientific analysis and observation is objectivity. The validity of any conclusion and the reliability of any observation are—or should be—independent of the values and beliefs of the scientist. Two plus two equals four, whether calculated by a Communist, a Catholic, a Moslem, or an African witch doctor. Women in the United States, as in most countries, live longer than men, a conclusion that both men and women should reach on the basis of the available data. The scientist tries to follow his data and the logic of his analysis wherever they may lead. Ideally, he keeps his philosophical views, political allegiances, religious beliefs, social preferences, and personal feelings from in any way influencing his results. He must avoid those biases that, in the words of Francis Bacon, a seventeenth-century advocate of an empirical approach to the study of nature, "so beset men's minds that truth can hardly find an entrance." (Bacon identified four kinds of biases, or *Idols,* as he called them: Idols of the Tribe, the limitations stemming from man's natural defects of understanding; of the Cave, the false notions an individual acquires from "education, habit and accident"; of the Marketplace, the confusions introduced by the nature of language; and of the Theater, ideas derived from philosophical systems and reasoning.[5])

Objectivity is likely to be far more difficult to achieve in all the social sciences than in the natural sciences, for men inevitably bring to their study of themselves and their society a body of ideas that may affect their observations and bias their conclusions. As psychologists have clearly demonstrated, men often see what they are prepared—or what they wish—to see. The facts to which they pay attention, or, more precisely, the phenomena in the world around them that they report as facts, are largely determined by the things they have learned, the beliefs to which they subscribe, the values they hold. Because men acquire, necessarily, a great number of ideas and opinions as they grow into adult members of a society, sociologists bring to their inquiries a set of preconceptions that they must eliminate or control in order to prevent biased observations or distorted interpretations of their findings.

No one can function as a member of society without some knowledge of how men behave, of the motives that drive them, of the prevailing customs and conventions. Indeed, such knowledge provides the substantial measure of predictability that enables men to live together without endless strife and difficulty. Consider merely how uncertain and confusing one's daily life would be if it were impossible to predict how students and teachers, bus drivers and store clerks, bank tellers and policemen, fathers and fiancées were going to act.

Such common-sense knowledge, however, can inhibit scientific inquiry, for it sometimes leads men to make questionable assumptions about human behavior, to interpret their findings in conformity with their opinions rather than with either facts or logic, or even to decry the very necessity for sociological study. The tendency to regard as natural what is widespread or conventional in one's own society, the view (called *ethnocentrism* by sociologists and anthropologists) that one's own group is the measure of man everywhere, constitutes a major obstacle to scientific objectivity. When peoples of the West were engaged in the relatively free and unfettered economic competition of nineteenth-century capitalism, it seemed only natural to economists that "the propensity to truck, barter and exchange" was an inherent element in human nature. Comparative evidence from many societies, however, runs counter to this assumption; the form and extent of economic exchange and the values placed upon it vary widely in different parts of the world. The alternative to projecting one's own standards, beliefs, and values upon others may, however, be the equally unwarranted conclusion that strange or foreign customs can only be unhuman and those who practice these customs are therefore actually less than human.

Because sociology frequently deals with the things with which men are familiar, and about which they do possess some common-sense knowledge, it has sometimes been labeled a science of the obvious, whose major activity consists in carefully documenting in elaborate detail, with tables of painstakingly gained statistics, what men already know. Clearly this criticism has no merit when one studies the unfamiliar, whether foreign or domestic. But it is a criticism most pointedly and frequently made when sociologists study things close to home—family life, reading habits, community organization, political practices.

The pursuit of reliable knowledge in a field where everyone is likely to feel that he already knows the answers inevitably exposes the sociologist to criticisms from many directions. As Robert K. Merton has pointed out:

> Should . . . systematic inquiry only confirm what has been widely assumed . . . [the sociologist] will of course be charged with "laboring the obvious." He becomes tagged as a bore, telling only what everybody knows. Should investigation find that widely held social beliefs are untrue . . . he is a heretic, questioning value-laden verities. If he ventures to examine socially implausible ideas that turn out to be untrue, he is a fool, wasting effort on a line of inquiry not worth pursuing in the first place. And finally, if he should turn up some implausible truths, he must be prepared to find himself regarded as a charlatan, claiming as knowledge what is patently false. Instances of each of these alternatives have occurred in the history of many sciences, but they would seem especially apt to occur in a discipline, such as sociology, that deals with matters about which men have firm opinions presumably grounded in their own experience.[6]

Sociologists, it is true, are occasionally so immersed in their endeavors that perspective is lost and any collection of information that is systematically assembled and leads to a generalization seems portentous, even when it only indicates that what we have always believed is true. But since common-sense knowledge is frequently flawed by inaccuracy and limited in its scope, particularly in a large and complex society, the sociologist's error lies not in testing conventional opinion but in reporting as a significant finding, frequently in pedantic, abstract language, what men already "know" to be true.

The extent of error in the taken-for-granted knowledge of Americans was clearly indicated by research conducted during World War II by the Army's Research Branch.[7] Such widely accepted notions as the following turned out to be false: that educated men were more likely to suffer psychological breakdown in military service than those with less education; that southern soldiers were better equipped to survive the rigors of tropical climate than northerners; that Negroes were less ambitious for promotion than whites; that men from rural backgrounds took army hardships better than city-reared soldiers. "That a belief is common . . . ," the American anthropologist Alfred L. Kroeber has observed, "is as likely to stamp it as a common superstition as a common truth." [8] Error, moreover, is frequently coupled with ignorance. How accurate a picture of the life of the poor and almost poor do those who live in comfortable middle-class suburbs possess? Do citizens on farms and in small towns, clerks in five-and-ten-cent stores, and workers in factories have a reliable view of the operations of centralized government? How much do college professors know about the world of business, or businessmen of the values and life of college professors? Yet each person believes that he knows, in some fashion and to some extent, how his society operates; indeed, as we have already pointed out, he must know something if he is to function effectively within it.

In seeking for the objectivity and reliability of science, one must not only exclude mere opinions as to facts and the relations that obtain among them, but one must also avoid the judgments and evaluations that may color men's thinking about themselves and their society. When Aristotle discussed the nature of civil society he not only offered explanations for what he saw, he also indicated, explicitly and implicitly, his own preferences. From the many social, or sociological, theories which have been developed in the course of human history, men have usually deduced or defended their own preferences in the organization of human society. As the eighteenth-century writer Bernard de Mandeville observed: "One of the greatest Reasons why so few People understand themselves, is that most Writers are always teaching Men what they should be, and hardly ever trouble their heads about what they really are." [9]

The distinction between careful description and analysis on the one hand and evaluation on the other, however, is not always clear, and the latter is frequently substituted for the former. It is perhaps easier to deprecate juvenile delinquency or a high divorce rate than to explain their existence; it is simpler to make political speeches lauding America as a land of opportunity than to try to assess how much opportunity exists, for whom it exists, and whether it is increasing or decreasing. The task of the sociologist, however, is not to judge, but to explain, not to argue for some given or desired state of affairs, but to examine the workings of society and the consequences which flow from alternative ways of doing things. "A moral judgment," Robert M. MacIver has said, "no matter how much we may agree with it, cannot be a substitute for the proper study of causes." [10]

It is no easy task for men to put aside their values and preconceptions, to see with the wise and innocent eyes of the boy who shouted: "But the Emperor has no clothes!" Men who expect women to be soft and emotional and find that most of the women they know do exhibit these qualities may not readily accept the possibility that these are not inherent feminine traits but may be the product of a particular kind of experience and education. Southerners who acquire, as they grow up, the belief in innate Negro inferiority find it difficult to accept the findings of modern research into racial differences. Those who believe that lack of ambition is a moral failing are reluctant to accept the view that it may result from lack of opportunity and encouragement.

Objectivity in sociology is difficult to achieve, but not impossible. The social changes that have made sociology both possible and desirable have also made it easier for men to become objective about the social life around them. Few nations now live in a state of stagnant isolation in which new ideas or challenges to accepted ways are rare or infrequent. Even totalitarian states find it difficult to choke off entirely the flow of communication from outside their boundaries. Men everywhere are now often, or even constantly, exposed to different values and customs that may lead them to look more dispassionately at their own. This is especially true if these new values command serious, even if critical, attention, though under some conditions the responses they engender inhibit rather than foster detachment and objectivity. When alien ways of life offer a strong challenge to established institutions and interests, men may refuse to examine their own practices and beliefs and will, instead, reject or deny the findings of those whose professional business it is to study the workings of society.

Scientific objectivity about man and society requires some understanding of one's own preferences and beliefs and can be substantially facilitated by the body of ideas— the concepts and theories—that one uses in making observations and in interpreting the data one collects. Objectivity, therefore, may be generated by sociological study itself. Familiarity with sociological data and systematic training in the nature and methods of sociological inquiry potentially make it possible both to control one's biases by becoming aware of them and to bypass one's preconceptions by approaching social phenomena from a different angle of vision. As we examine the structure and functioning of other societies we may achieve a clearer perspective about our own. As we analyze our society we may perhaps see ourselves more clearly in relation to the world in which we live.

Science and concepts: the problem of jargon

We have thus far not defined sociology, other than to identify it as a scientific study of man and society. But this statement tells us what sociology is about, not what it is or how it differs from anthropology, psychology, economics, political science, and history, all of which also study man and society. To offer a definition at this point in order to isolate the essential ingredients in sociology and to distinguish it from the other social sciences would be of little value. We might define sociology as the study of human groups, of social relationships, of social institutions, or, perhaps more elaborately, as "the science which attempts to develop an analytical theory of social action systems in so far as these systems can be understood in terms of the property of common-value integration." [11] But we should understand these definitions only after we had explored the meaning of the key terms or concepts, that is, the meaning of "groups," "social relationships," "social institutions," and "social action systems" and "common-value integration." In so doing we should also necessarily introduce still other terms whose meaning we should then have to define.

The first step toward the understanding of sociology, as of any scientific discipline, is the mastery of its basic concepts. We referred earlier to "the things in the world around them that men report as facts." What men see, we noted, depends upon what they expect to see, what they look for. Their expectations are defined by the categories, or concepts, with which they think. Ideas, after all, are the tools with which we organize and interpret what we see and hear and do.

The concepts of sociology, then, provide the intellectual instruments with which the sociologist works. They define the phenomena to be studied, and they differentiate sociology from the other social sciences, each of which has its own body of concepts. They focus attention upon those selected aspects of reality with which we shall be concerned, and they provide the terms in which problems are posed and answered.

The concepts we shall present, it must be noted, though basic to sociological inquiry, do not exhaust the conceptual arsenal used by the sociologist. In dealing with the various areas and forms of social life—the family, religion, social stratification, power and authority, large-scale organization, and so on—it is necessary to supplement the broad categories which define the sociological perspective with more limited and more specific concepts.

In devoting a large part of this book to an exposition of concepts and the definition of key terms, we expose ourselves to a frequently made charge that we are merely creating and manipulating a distinctive jargon which adds little to human understanding. We may be taxed with using familiar terms in unfamiliar ways, with offering what seem to be esoteric labels for otherwise familiar phenomena; in sum, with creating an unusual and unnecessary terminology. In part, of course, this criticism is another reflection of the common-sense approach to the understanding of man and society. Yet this is a criticism that must be examined before we proceed.

First, it is important to observe that this complaint is

rarely leveled with the same critical animus against the natural sciences, whose learned journals are almost completely impenetrable to the nonprofessional. It is clearly not the existence of a distinctive vocabulary that provokes criticism, but the nature of the field and its relationship to human life.

Since sociology deals with many of the ordinary features of social life, there appears to the layman to be little need for distinctive terminology or for careful definition of terms he himself frequently uses. As we have noted, any member of a society knows something about its workings. Everyone can provide a plausible and reasonable explanation for many of the actions of people with whom he associates, or of whom he hears. Both behavior and the reasons for it can be described in everyday language, as can the organization of groups with which each man is familiar or in which he participates. When the student of human behavior applies special terms to commonplace actions and substitutes for common-sense explanations statements that include in many instances unfamiliar and high-sounding words, the sensibilities of the outsider are offended. When common-sense explanations are not available, many persons are likely to deny the possibility of any explanation, scientific or otherwise. "Free will" or "the uniqueness of the individual" or some other phrase is called upon to justify this denial of the possibility of understanding and explanation.

Second, the fruits of scientific social research are not yet so rich or so widely known that its peculiar terminology will be accepted just as that of the natural sciences has been accepted. Of course, its practical application is not the sole test of the value of social science; its contribution to knowledge and understanding is in itself justification for its existence. Nevertheless, it is probably true that only when the social scientist can demonstrate that he can successfully contribute directly to the welfare of his society will the public accept without question or criticism his freedom to speak in his own private language to the professionals in his field.

To the extent that sociology creates a language for professional use, it will probably be necessary to develop simultaneously a corps of popularizers similar to those who present the findings of natural science to the public in terms that the intelligent layman can understand. Such a corps of popularizers appears to be already in the making. Although popular writers need possess no professional qualifications and therefore differ widely in their ability to present adequately the findings of serious scholars, they will inevitably have considerable influence—for good or for ill—upon the public image and repute of sociology. Some sociologists may, of course, perform a dual role—as researcher and as popularizer. But to insist that every sociologist must confine himself to language that can be understood by any intelligent person is probably to impose an insuperable handicap upon the development of social science.

Third, there is also a perhaps understandable suspicion of the man who tries to study others as objectively as the lepidopterist studies butterflies or the ichthyologist studies fish. Since knowledge can be power, men are sometimes distrustful of those who know too much and can talk about human beings and their behavior in a language that cannot readily be understood. Those who lack power are fearful of a potential new wielder of influence or control. Those who already occupy important positions or possess vested interests in society are likely to be hostile to men who may either directly or indirectly offer a challenge to their privileges and perquisites by analyzing the nature of their power. Since men are usually deeply committed to their own ways of life, looking upon them not only as natural and inevitable but also as morally right, they tend to offer staunch resistance to any questioning or analysis that seeks to explain their ways of life in scientific terms, for such an explanation seems to question both their inevitability and their moral propriety.

Yet the criticism of sociological jargon is sometimes warranted. There are undoubtedly a good many instances in which sociologists have been guilty of the overuse or unnecessary use of special terminology (a sin we shall try to avoid). We may attribute excessive jargon to the enthusiasm of fresh practitioners in the field or of those caught up in the excitement generated in what is, after all, a relatively new and rapidly growing field. In part, too, jargon is a result of efforts of a young discipline to mark out its area of study and to achieve academic respectability.

Despite its abuses, however, we cannot do away with distinctive, sharply defined terminology. The usual ambiguities of everyday language can be avoided only by insisting upon the precise use of words. When new ideas emerge it is frequently necessary to find new terms with which to identify them.

The nature of concepts

Before we can examine the basic sociological concepts it is necessary to define more clearly the nature of concepts and to explain and illustrate why they are so important. Put most simply, a concept is a general term that refers to all members of a particular class of objects, events, persons, relationships, processes, ideas. Everyone frequently uses concepts. Like the much-cited hero of Molière's *Le Bourgeois Gentilhomme* who found that he had been speaking prose only after he had been doing so for forty years, we have all used concepts ever since we learned to talk. Learning to use language and to think entails the growth of an ability to employ general rather than specific terms and ideas, to think of "toys" rather than of a particular toy, of "boys" rather than of the boy next door, of "water" rather than of a particular thirst-quenching drink. As the distinguished French sociologist Émile Durkheim pointed out: "The system of concepts with which we think in everyday life is that expressed by the vocabulary of our mother tongue; for every word translates a concept." [12]

If our ordinary conversation constantly utilizes concepts, what are the differences between them and the concepts of science? The latter are both more precisely defined and more abstract or general in their application. In daily conversation the meaning of the words we use is taken for granted; we assume that others know what we are saying. For most purposes this assumption is safe enough, even though many words have more than one meaning. The appropriate meaning is indicated in each case by the specific context, verbal or social, in which the term is used. If we talk about our "family," for example, we may be referring to our parents, brothers, and sisters (what the sociologists call the "nuclear family"), or to all our kinfolk; the meaning will normally be made clear by the conversation in which the word appears.

Many commonly used terms have no precise meaning, nor can they be understood from the contexts in which they do appear. If we try to set up precise and generally acceptable definitions of communism, subversion, liberalism, loyalty, or freedom, or of such nonpolitical terms as friendship, success, and ambition, we will quickly see that for these words there is no simple meaning upon which most people agree. As students of semantics have frequently pointed out, many words, particularly the "big ones," are often used more for their emotional value than for any concrete meaning they may have. Like the fisherman's "big ones," they often elude capture, and their meaning is as reliable as the fisherman's tale. But our language serves not only to communicate ideas, but also, by the overtones of many words, to indicate feelings and attitudes and even on occasion to

suggest possible courses of action. (There are some se-
manticists who argue that the source of many of the social
and political problems we face lies in the confusions created
by a nonscientific language, or, in Bacon's terms, by the
Idols of the Marketplace. It is unlikely, however, that eliminating semantic confusion would eliminate our problems,
for there exist in society real conflicts of interest and concrete difficulties engendered by existing institutions.)

Since science requires rigorous logical analysis as well
as careful objective observation, the meaning of the terms
which it uses must be as clear and precise as possible, independent of different contexts and free from ambiguities and
complex overtones. Unlike those disciplines which have
escaped from the liabilities of the language of everyday
discourse by utilizing a mathematical terminology or by
coining new words whenever necessary, sociology has on
the whole developed a vocabulary based upon terms current
in popular usage. Such common words as *culture, group,*
role, status, power, authority, function, race, and *bureauc-*
racy have become important sociological concepts. Their
definition requires the analysis of the things to which they
refer—in semantic terminology, their *referents*. (In philosophical terminology, the definitions of sociological concepts must be real and not nominal definitions, that is, they
must identify the central elements in the phenomenon being analyzed rather than being merely an "agreement or
resolution concerning the use of verbal symbols." [13])

The concepts of sociology, like those of any science, refer
to types or classes of events, persons, and relationships—for
example, to revolutions or doctors, to cooperation or conflict. Much, if not most, of our everyday conversation, on
the other hand, deals with specific individuals, occasions,
situations, and material things. We talk of our family, our
jobs, our relationship with a member of the opposite sex.
We spend little time considering in general terms the nature of the family, of jobs, or of dating. The task of so-

ciology, as of all sciences, is to analyze classes of phenomena, not individual cases. The sociologist will be concerned with divorce in a particular family or with a revolution at a particular time and place in order to throw light on the nature of divorce or of revolutions as types of social phenomena. In the long run—and this is a major contribution of sociology—the deeper our understanding of divorce or revolution or other social phenomena in general, the greater is apt to be our understanding of specific instances.

Concepts are derived or created by *abstracting* selected aspects or features of phenomena from the total complexity of reality. Despite its formidable label—abstraction—this process is not a purely esoteric exercise, for it is frequently, if unwittingly, pursued by most of us. As Cohen and Nagel point out:

> All thinking proceeds by noting certain distinguishable features in things, symbolizing such selected features by appropriate counters, and then reasoning upon such abstracted features by means of the symbols. In dealing intellectually with some concrete, specific situation, we do not pay attention to all the infinitely complex relations which it has, or to all of its qualities. On the contrary, we neglect almost all of the qualities and relations which a thing has, and note only those features which enable us to view that thing as an instance or example of indefinitely repeatable patterns or types of situations. Thus our knowledge of things involves abstraction from the infinitely complex and perhaps unique properties which situations have.[14]

Although concepts are sometimes called "constructs," thus emphasizing the fact that they are creations of human thought and not necessarily inherent in the nature of social reality, it is important to be aware of the fact that they are not simply arbitrary products of inquiring and imaginative minds. They may refer to purely hypothetical processes or entities which cannot be directly observed or experienced, such as atoms in physics, the ego in psychology, or institutions in sociology. Yet even these highly abstract concepts emerge from some kind of observation of experience; they represent efforts to impose some kind of intellectual order upon the flux and diversity of life. Because concepts stem from the interplay of imagination and observation we shall try to suggest, as we introduce and make use of the categories of sociology, the nature of the observations from which they derive.

The uses of concepts

Concepts, then, lead us to look for patterns or regularities or uniformities in the world around us. We are seeking for that feature or aspect of a particular family which is similar to the features of other families, for the attributes shared by men as members of a group, or for the forms of organization which characterize collective activities. We are not concerned with the idiosyncratic, or the peculiar, which intrigues the creative writer or frequently the historian, but with those repetitive patterns which eventually can be distinguished as we observe the behavior of men and women in society.

To seek for patterns or regularities is not, as sometimes charged, to deny uniqueness or individuality. Any process of generalization ignores those characteristics that distinguish one individual from another, whether it be an individual person, volcano, or atomic explosion. In ignoring the unique qualities of any of these single entities, it may appear that science denies their existence. This is simply not true. Nor is there a necessary conflict between an interest in the unique and a concern with repetitive features of life or nature. They constitute alternative ways of paying attention to the world around us, each with its own distinctive values, and each contributing something to the other.

Sociology's interest in the "group" has sometimes been contrasted with psychology's emphasis upon the "individual," as if only the former dealt with recurrent aspects of human life. In this case the antithesis between the general and the particular does not apply; both disciplines are concerned with patterns or regularities—sociology with those to be found in the relations of individuals and groups to one another and in the structure and functioning of groups, psychology with those uniformities to be discovered in the structure and functioning of individual personalities. (We shall have more to say of the differences—and relations—between these two disciplines in Chapter 4.)

In defining the concepts of sociology then, we are setting forth the nature and limits of the sociological perspective. Our concepts focus attention upon those selected aspects of reality with which we shall be concerned. In effect, they also distinguish sociology from the other social sciences, each of which, because of its own perspective, sees different aspects of the same social phenomena. We can perhaps illustrate this point very simply. Eating a slice of buttered toast for breakfast can be analyzed in terms of the nutritive value of the food consumed, the eating habits of individuals, the economics of the bread, dairy, and home appliance industries, conventional or customary dietary patterns, or even as a possible source of social friction because the wife does not make the toast dark enough to suit her husband's taste. The key words in each case—"nutritive value," "individual habits," "economics of industries," "conventional or customary patterns," and "social friction"—are drawn from different disciplines: nutrition, psychology, economics, and sociology. The student in each field will use his own categories and will usually disregard the possibility that the same event might also be looked at from other points of view. (There is often, of course, some overlapping in the perspectives of the several social sciences, and concepts in one discipline are often used—and sometimes misused—by workers in another.)

By focusing attention upon selected aspects of reality concepts in effect tell us what to look at. But they also tell us what to look *for* when we approach specific empirical questions. For example, if we wished to explain the existence of delinquent gangs of teen-agers, our general concepts would guide our search for factors that might be relevant. As sociologists we would collect data to see whether delinquent gangs drew their members from all *social classes,* all *ethnic groups,* and all types of *communities,* or whether delinquency was equally frequent in all the various kinds of *social groups.* We would try to see what *cultural values* were involved in this form of *deviant behavior* and would explore the distinctive features of the teen-ager's *roles* in whatever groups the gangs were drawn from. We would examine the *social relationships* within the gang and its relations to other groups and *institutions.*[15] The italicized terms illustrate the concepts with which the sociologist operates. He need not know much about delinquent gangs when he starts; he assumes on the basis of much evidence and past experience that these general concepts probably will lead him to the specific factors relevant to the problem.

The use of abstract concepts makes possible the derivation of generalizations relevant to a wide range of observations. Deviant behavior, for example, refers not only to delinquency, but also to political corruption, cheating on examinations, philandering, and any other activities which run counter to accepted social standards. Similarly the term *bureaucracy* has been defined so that it includes elements of social structure found not only in government, but in banks, insurance companies, factories, labor unions, universities, veterans' associations, and other large organizations. Analysis of the range of phenomena included in these general categories will obviously yield broader generalizations than would be obtainable if each form of deviant behavior or of bureaucratic organization were considered separately. Since the goal of science is a body of theory covering the widest possible range of phenomena, from which inferences may then be drawn about specific cases, some sociological concepts will tend, as the science grows, toward a constantly higher level of abstraction.

So significant a part of sociology are its concepts that the history of the discipline is in part a history of conceptual elaboration and refinement. Many concepts have been suggested for organizing and analyzing social phenomena. Some have come into general use whereas others have gained currency for a time, only to be displaced by more precise or more refined categories of observation and analysis. There is usually little question of the truth or falsity of a concept, although it is possible for one to be wrong. To say that men are quadrupedal mammals is obviously false since we know what men look like and how they get about. Or to say that a family consists only of the mother and her children runs counter to our accumulated observations of family life. But in most cases where alternative concepts are available the choice usually depends upon which one is more useful in accounting for the facts being scrutinized.

Considerable difference of opinion still exists among sociologists about which concepts should be used and how they should be defined. For example, Talcott Parsons, one of the major contemporary theorists, has formulated a set of categories for analyzing social systems and social action that he identifies as the "pattern variables," but many other writers make little use of his ideas. Some sociologists emphasize *ecological* concepts, those having to do with the relationship between the community and the habitat (the biological and physical environment), but others pay little attention to these categories. In addition to such conceptual differences there is also some degree of terminological disorder; we will find, for instance, that the terms society, culture, institution, social structure, and status are used to refer to various kinds of sociological phenomena and, conversely, that the same phenomenon is on occasion given different labels.

Disagreement and inconsistency, while frequently inconvenient and confusing, are not unique to sociology; they exist, although in varying degrees, in every field. In each discipline there is continuing testing and refinement of the many alternative concepts that scholars offer for use in the competitive market of ideas. The extent of conceptual differences in sociology is in part a product of its rapid development. Many still valuable works written in the past, even the relatively recent past, use concepts that have since been refined or replaced by more precise terms. As the volume and tempo of research increase, the inadequacies of present concepts become more readily apparent, and new categories are frequently required to deal with fresh data and new distinctions. Although there has been an increasing consensus within sociology, we cannot look forward to an end of the process of conceptual analysis and clarification, for this process is an inherent and persisting feature of any scientific discipline.

These facts require that the presentation of concepts in the following chapters include not only the definitions to be used in this book but also, in certain instances, a review of alternative usages. Any definition is in part arbitrary; the essential requirement is consistency of usage. Consistency, however, is sometimes confined only to a particular context; the same term may apply to different, though usually related, aspects of social life. Culture, for example, may refer to the whole way of life of a society or, more narrowly, to that segment of a way of life that encompasses values, knowledge, beliefs, and symbols. Which meaning is intended will usually emerge from the context, or it will be made explicit. (For a full discussion of culture, see Chapter 2.)

Science and theory

Concepts alone do not constitute a discipline; they merely provide the building blocks with which a science, as a body of substantive knowledge, is constructed. In approaching the analysis of specific problems more is required than the awareness of potentially relevant variables furnished by a conceptual apparatus. Nor is the end result of scientific inquiry merely the categorizing and classification of social phenomena, however important and necessary these steps may be. The goal of science is the building of theory, a body of logically interrelated propositions that assert determinate relations among the phenomena being studied.

The nature of sociological theory can be illustrated in the following example:

(1) Men tend to behave according to the expectations of others.

(2) If men change their associates they are likely, therefore, to acquire the attitudes and behavior of those with whom they have recently established social relationships.

(3a) It might therefore be expected that if northerners with little bias toward Negroes move to the Deep South they will in time acquire southern racial attitudes and conform to southern racial customs, since their new associates will expect such attitudes and actions. (John Dollard, a northern sociologist and social psychologist who studied a southern community, has commented: "The development of attitudes appropriate to a changed reality is nicely illustrated by the behavior of white outsiders who come into Southern-town and become permanent residents. They soon take over, it is said, the attitudes proper to their caste and class toward the Negro. My own observation tends to bear out this statement." [16] The "changed reality," of course, includes the differing expectations of those permanent residents with whom the newcomer necessarily associates.)

(3b) The rate and extent of this change, however, will

depend upon whether they associate chiefly with southerners or with other migrant northerners.

(4a) Similarly, southerners with prevailing southern attitudes toward Negroes are likely to change their racial attitudes and behavior if they move to the North.

(4b) But, again, the rate and extent of change will depend upon whether they associate chiefly with other migrants like themselves, with northerners who share their views, or with northerners with little bias toward the Negro.[17]

There is interesting experimental evidence for the broad generalizations of which propositions 3a, 3b, 4a, and 4b are specific examples, namely, that men's attitudes and judgments tend to conform to those of the group of which they are a part, but that dissident views can be sustained if they are shared by others, even if only a minority. In an experiment by Solomon Asch, each person in a group was asked to compare the length of a particular line with one of three other lines of different lengths. All but one of the group were primed to give incorrect answers. The unknowing subjects tended to change their judgments to conform to those of the others, despite the fact that objectively the latter were wrong. But when two unknowing subjects were in the group, they apparently sustained one another, for they refused to change their judgments to conform to the erroneous answers of the others.[18]

All of the propositions in this example of sociological theory suffer from overgeneralization, for they ignore important variables and fail to specify the conditions under which they would hold true, or might require modification. For example, the intensity with which men hold to their opinions will affect their responsiveness to the expectations of others and therefore their susceptibility to change. It is probable that southerners are more deeply committed to their attitudes toward Negroes than are white northerners; the latter would therefore be more prone to change their opinions and behavior under changing circumstances than would southerners. Further, people are more likely to take into account the opinions of those about whose judgments they are concerned—for whatever reasons: love, respect, fear, or expediency—than the expectations of persons about whose opinions they do not care.

Despite such limitations, these propositions can serve to demonstrate the nature of theory and the elements of which it is composed, and its uses and value as well. The extent to which concepts are utilized should be obvious; expectations of others, customary associates, migrants, northerners, southerners, rate of change, attitudes, and customs are all general categories, each of which includes numerous specific items. Without them description and analysis would be impossible. But the theoretical significance of these concepts lies in the relationships which can be established among the variables they represent.

The six propositions are all logically related; the pairs, 3a and 3b, and 4a and 4b, can be derived logically from the initial, more general statements. This logical development is possible because some of the concepts are inclusive of others; migrants, for example, include both northerners and southerners who move, and the concept of the "expectations of others" obviously has very wide reference. The six propositions clearly vary in their scope and generality; the first two are extremely broad, the following two pairs much more limited in their applicability. If the latter had been elaborated they would have led to the formulation of empirical generalizations, that is, of propositions that summarize "observed uniformities of relationships between two or more variables." [19] In this case the generalizations would be of the following order:

> More northerners who move to the South and acquire southern friends change their attitudes toward Negroes than do migrant northerners who associate chiefly with others of

a similar background. (This assumes that their attitudes are originally similar and not "anti-Negro.")

Fewer southerners who move to Detroit, where they are very numerous, change their attitudes toward Negroes than do southerners who move to a city where such migrants are few in number.

We can represent the first of these propositions in the following tabular form:

	Those whose attitudes change	Those whose attitudes do not change	Total
Migrants from the North who associate with native southerners	$A(\%)$	$B(\%)$	$X(100\%)$
Migrants from the North who associate with other migrants	$C(\%)$	$D(\%)$	$Y(100\%)$

If the presumed relationship between social relationships and change of attitude obtains for northern migrants, then A should be a larger proportion of X than C is of Y; conversely, B should be a smaller proportion of X than D is of Y; or, to use hypothetical figures, 70 per cent of migrants who associate with natives might change their attitudes toward Negroes, compared with, say, 35 per cent of those who associate chiefly with one another. Whether this difference is significant in any given research would depend upon the number of persons who were studied, and how they were selected. The value of this schematic formulation lies in its statement of the kind of statistical data needed in order to ascertain the validity of empirical generalizations. Empirical propositions of this sort, which merely assert that two things occur together, constitute both the evidence for general theoretical propositions and the facts to be explained by theory.

Sociology contains a great many empirical generalizations, and research continues to add to their number. Rural families are usually larger than urban families. Divorce occurs less frequently among men and women with college education than among those with less education. Poor people spend proportionately more of their income for food than do wealthy people. Delinquent gangs are more commonly found in slum areas of cities than in middle- or upper-class areas. More women migrate from farms to cities than men. And so on. The task of sociology is to account for empirical generalizations such as these and to incorporate them into a system of general propositions, or theory.

The value of theory stems from its inclusiveness and generality. As soon as some action or event or situation can be conceptualized and placed into a category whose relationship to other variables is known, it becomes possible to draw useful inferences. What applies to southern or northern migrants may hold for farmers who move to the city, for urbanites who move to the suburbs, and for successful men who move from New York City's lower east side to the upper east side. (This bypasses, of course, the possibility that migration may occur after attitudes and behavior have changed rather than before; migration itself may result from antecedent changes in the persons who move. In any empirical study it would be essential to know the attitudes and practices existing before men moved in order to be able to assess both the changes that occur afterward and the reasons for such changes.) Theory is then both economical and informative, since statements can be made about an individual case or about an empirical generalization without necessarily investigating it in great detail. Each of these inferences, of course, must usually be tested in research, for it is possible that other relevant circumstances may affect the relationships between the variables.

By identifying the conditions under which events are likely to occur, theory makes possible prediction and perhaps some measure of control. Such predictions, it should be remembered, are not forecasts. They do not assert that something will in fact happen, but only that *if* certain conditions exist it is likely to happen. The birth rate will probably rise, for example, if the age of marriage goes down, or if the proportion of women in the child-bearing ages who are married goes up. One could only forecast a rise in the birth rate if one knew that the age of marriage was declining or that the proportion of married women among those in the 15-to-45-year-old group was rising.

It is necessary to emphasize the practical value of theory, for abstract and generalized knowledge about social life and human behavior is often contrasted invidiously with the "practical" approach of the man of affairs; the presumed sterility of "ivory-tower thinking" is set against the apparent productivity of the activities of the businessman, the practical politician, the organizer and executive; the knowledge-oriented researches of the social scientist are looked upon as of little value when compared with the action-oriented efforts of the social worker or town planner or social reformer. At a time when the fruitfulness of abstract scientific theory is so eloquently illustrated in each nuclear explosion and orbiting earth satellite, it seems hardly necessary to reiterate the fact that scientific theory can, in the long run, be eminently practical, far more so, indeed, than presumably time-tested practices and common sense. And yet when one deals with theories of man and society it is necessary to repeat this important lesson. So contained are most men in their immediate social context and so committed to the prevailing common-sense interpretations of behavior and events that abstract generalizations are not readily accepted.

It is sometimes said in criticism of theory that it narrows or limits what men see, for it confines their vision to those variables incorporated in the theory and therefore prevents them from seeking other and frequently important facts. Obviously this claim is true: In paying attention to some aspects of reality we necessarily disregard or ignore others. This is not a fatal criticism, however, for science is inherently self-correcting. No theory is ever final, and as new and unexplained facts appear it becomes necessary to revise what was heretofore accepted. Further, sociology is not an exclusive road to understanding. Nor does it deny the validity or desirability of other roads, scientific or otherwise. Sociology is one road among others, although in our modern, complex society it can be one of great significance and value.

The value of sociology

Sociology, both as tested theory and as a body of reliable facts, possesses a double value: It can add to man's understanding of himself and his society, and it can contribute to solutions of problems he faces in achieving and maintaining the kind of society in which he hopes to live. We have already referred to the limitations of common-sense knowledge. In a rapidly changing world, such knowledge inevitably becomes unreliable, both as a source of understanding and as a guide to action. Traditional explanations that may once have been reasonably accurate no longer apply as circumstances change. The increasing complexity of modern society creates problems for which there are no ready-made answers. In this situation sociology constitutes a useful, even essential, source of reliable knowledge for both the individual and society.

The relevance of sociology to many of the problems faced by society and its constituent parts hardly needs elaboration. Surely, reliable facts are more useful than hearsay or untested generalizations, and a systematic understanding of cause and effect, of the relations among facts,

is a better guide to action than the uncertain results of
trial and error or the unreliable precepts handed down by
tradition. And yet the lesson presented long ago by Herbert Spencer in a much-cited passage needs continually to
be repeated:

> You see that this wrought-iron plate is not quite flat: it
> sticks up a little here towards the left—"cockles," as we say.
> How shall we flatten it? Obviously, you reply, by hitting
> down on the part that is prominent. Well, here is a hammer,
> and I give the plate a blow as you advise. Harder, you say.
> Still no effect. Another stroke? Well, there is one, and an-
> other, and another. The prominence remains, you see: the
> evil is as great as ever—greater, indeed. But this is not all.
> Look at the warp which the plate has got near the opposite
> edge. Where it was flat before it is now curved. A pretty
> bungle we have made of it. Instead of curing the original
> defect, we have produced a second. Had we asked an artisan
> practiced in "planishing," as it is called, he would have told
> us that no good was to be done, but only mischief, by hitting
> down on the projecting part. He would have taught us how
> to give variously-directed and specially-adjusted blows with a
> hammer elsewhere: so attacking the evil not by direct but by
> indirect actions. The required process is less simple than you
> thought. Even a sheet of metal is not to be successfully dealt
> with after those common-sense methods in which you have so
> much confidence. What, then, shall we say about a society?
> "Do you think I am easier to be played on than a pipe?" asks
> Hamlet. Is humanity more readily straightened than an iron
> plate? [20]

In its origins sociology was frequently considered to be
an instrument for dealing with social "evils." Increasingly
it now seems to be providing an approach and point of
view useful in interpreting and understanding the complex
and difficult world in which we live. Despite frequent criticisms of sociology—its jargon, methods, and ideas—critics,

novelists, historians, and others are making widespread use of its perspectives and findings.

The hopes and aspirations of any discipline almost inevitably outrun its achievements. Humanity, even with a fully developed social science as its instrument, is not likely to "straighten" itself, and sociology is as yet an exceedingly imperfect tool. But "the sociological imagination," to use C. Wright Mills' hopeful phrase,

> is a quality of mind that seems most dramatically to promise an understanding of the intimate realities of ourselves in connection with larger social realities. It is not merely one quality of mind among the contemporary range of cultural sensibilities—it is the quality whose wider and more adroit use offers the promise that all such sensibilities—and in fact, human reason itself—will come to play a greater role in human affairs.[21]

Notes

[1] See, for example, Russell Kirk, "Is Social Science Scientific?" *The New York Times Magazine,* June 25, 1961, pp. 11 ff. For a rejoinder, see Robert K. Merton, "The Canons of the Anti-Sociologist," *The New York Times Magazine,* July 16, 1961, pp. 14 ff. Both articles are reprinted in Milton L. Barron (ed.), *Contemporary Sociology* (New York: Dodd, Mead, 1964), pp. 29–35, 35–40.

[2] For a discussion of the spread of interest in sociology in other countries, see Edward Shils, "The Calling of Sociology," in Talcott Parsons *et al.* (eds.), *Theories of Society,* II (New York: Free Press, 1961), 1405–9.

[3] Alfred N. Whitehead, *Science and the Modern World* (Cambridge, Eng.: Cambridge University Press, 1946), Ch. 1.

4 Ralph G. Ross, *Symbols and Civilization* (New York: Harcourt, 1962), p. 1.

5 For an early but still useful discussion of the biases that get in the way of objective sociological inquiry, see Herbert Spencer, *The Study of Sociology,* originally published in 1873 and republished in many editions.

6 Robert K. Merton, "Notes on Problem-Finding in Sociology," in Robert K. Merton, Leonard Broom, and Leonard S. Cottrell, Jr. (eds.), *Sociology Today* (New York: Basic Books, 1959), pp. xv–xvi *n.*

7 See Paul F. Lazarsfeld, *"The American Soldier:* An Expository Review," *Public Opinion Quarterly,* XIII (Fall, 1949), 377–404.

8 Alfred L. Kroeber, *The Nature of Culture* (Chicago: University of Chicago Press, 1952), p. 27.

9 Bernard de Mandeville, *The Fable of the Bees* (London: 1723), p. 25.

10 Robert M. MacIver, *Social Causation* (Boston: Ginn, 1942), p. 148.

11 Talcott Parsons, *The Structure of Social Action* (New York: McGraw-Hill, 1937), p. 768.

12 Émile Durkheim, *The Elementary Forms of the Religious Life,* trans. J. W. Swain (New York: Free Press, 1947), p. 433.

13 Morris R. Cohen and Ernest Nagel, *An Introduction to Logic and the Scientific Method* (New York: Harcourt, 1934), pp. 224–31. For an excellent discussion of definitions in sociology, see Robert Bierstedt, "Nominal and Real Definitions in Sociological Theory," in Llewellyn Gross (ed.), *Symposium on Sociological Theory* (Evanston: Row, Peterson, 1959), pp. 121–44.

14 *Ibid.,* p. 371.

15 For sophisticated sociological analyses of delinquent gangs, see Albert K. Cohen, *Delinquent Boys* (New York: Free Press, 1955); and Richard A. Cloward and Lloyd E. Ohlin, *Delinquency and Opportunity* (New York: Free Press, 1960).

[16] John Dollard, *Caste and Class in a Southern Town* (Garden City: Doubleday Anchor Books, 1957), p. 17. Dollard also notes the relevance of this tendency for research: "Undoubtedly many researchers who have gone South . . . have been seduced by the hospitality of the middle- and upper-class southern white people, have formed agreeable ties with them, and have thereupon been pulled into the southern mode of perception of the racial problem" (p. 37).

[17] For an analysis of the racial attitudes of some southerners who move north, see Lewis M. Killian, "The Effects of Southern White Workers on Race Relations in Northern Plants," *American Sociological Review,* XVII (June, 1952), 327–31.

[18] See Solomon Asch, "Effects of Group Pressure upon the Modification and Distortion of Judgments," in Eleanor E. Maccoby, Theodore M. Newcomb, and Eugene L. Hartley (eds.), *Readings in Social Psychology* (3rd ed.; New York: Holt, 1958), pp. 174–83.

[19] Robert K. Merton, *Social Theory and Social Structure* (rev. ed.; New York: Free Press, 1957), p. 95.

[20] Herbert Spencer, *The Study of Sociology* (10th ed.; London: Routledge, 1882), pp. 270–1. In 1936 Karl Mannheim, one of the leading and most influential sociologists, wrote: "For it is surely a striking commentary on the age in which we live, that whilst should any one try to repair his car without knowing the first thing about its machinery he would by common consent be dubbed a fool, yet no such derision is displayed toward those who, possessing no clear knowledge of cause and effect, believe that hitches in the mechanism of society can be set right by emotional resentments or irrational movements against social forces." "The Place of Sociology" in *The Social Sciences: Their Relations in Theory and Teaching* (London: LePlay, 1936), p. 164.

[21] C. Wright Mills, *The Sociological Imagination* (New York: Oxford, 1959), p. 15. For a useful discussion of the contribution of sociology to a general education, see Robert Bierstedt, "Sociology and General Education," in Charles H. Page (ed.), *Sociology and Contemporary Education* (New York: Random House, 1964), pp. 40–55.

Suggestions for further reading

BIERSTEDT, ROBERT. "Nominal and Real Definitions in Sociological Theory," in Llewellyn Gross (ed.), *Symposium on Sociological Theory.* Evanston: Row, Peterson, 1959, pp. 121–44.
An enlightening discussion of definitions in sociology that clears up a considerable amount of theoretical confusion and controversy. Written with a felicity of style characteristic of this distinguished sociologist.

MILLS, C. WRIGHT. *The Sociological Imagination.* New York: Oxford, 1959, Ch. 1, "The Promise."
An important statement on the cultural role of social science in the modern world.

PAGE, CHARLES H. (ed.). *Sociology and Contemporary Education.* New York: Random House, 1964.
A collection of essays on the intellectual and cultural contributions of sociology.

PARSONS, TALCOTT. "Some Problems Confronting Sociology as a Profession," *American Sociological Review,* XXIV (August, 1959), 547–59.
A recent statement by a leading sociologist on the present status of sociology as a profession and on its uses and prospects.

ROSS, RALPH. *Symbols and Civilization.* New York: Harcourt, 1962.
An excellent brief discussion of the nature of science, its methods, and its applicability to the study of society.

SPENCER, HERBERT. *The Study of Sociology.* First published in 1873 and republished in many editions.
A still useful analysis of the sources of bias in sociological inquiry.

THOMLINSON, RALPH. *Sociological Concepts and Research.* New York: Random House, 1965.
A brief and useful "survey of how modern sociologists go about their daily chores."

society and culture

Patterned behavior and collective life

Sociology begins with two basic facts: The behavior of human beings shows regular and recurrent patterns, and human beings are social animals and not isolated creatures.

The fundamental events of birth, death, and marriage, the private details of bathing, eating, and love-making, the public occurrences of vote-getting and producing or selling goods, and the myriad other activities in which men engage usually follow recognizable patterns. We often lose sight of the repetitive nature of most social action, however, for when we observe those persons around us we are more likely to notice their idiosyncrasies and personal quirks than their similarities. But if we compare ourselves with Frenchmen or Japanese or Trobriand Islanders we find ourselves saying: We do it this way; they do it that way. Charles

Horton Cooley, one of America's first important sociologists, once observed:

> Is it not the case that the nearer a thing is to our habit of thought the more clearly we see the individual . . . ? The principle is much the same as that which makes all [Chinese] look pretty much alike to us: we see the type because it is so different from what we are used to, but only one who lives within it can fully perceive the differences among individuals.[1]

In studying ourselves as we might study the Chinese or any other society different from our own, we abstract the recurrent features of behavior from the unique. When men respond to a personal introduction with a standardized phrase—"How do you do?"—the intonation, the tone, the volume may vary, but the verbal formulation remains the same. Some people shake hands energetically, with a strong grasp, while others have a limp and flabby handshake; these personal differences have significance in the social interchange which takes place, but they do not deny the existence of the patterned form of behavior which recurs when people meet.

The repeated aspects of human action are the basis for any social science. Without ascertainable patterns there could be no science, for generalization would be impossible. Sociology is distinguished from economics, political science, and psychology by the particular patterns it studies and how it looks at them. Those features of behavior upon which sociology focuses its attention are derived from the second basic fact upon which the discipline rests—the social character of human life.

"Man," wrote Aristotle more than two thousand years ago, "is naturally a political animal [in modern terms the word usually translated as *political* might more appropriately be translated as *social*] and . . . whosoever is naturally and not artificially unfit for society must be either inferior or superior to men." Adam Ferguson, an eighteenth-century Scottish moral philosopher, once observed in terms which are still appropriate: "Both the earliest and the latest accounts collected from every quarter of the earth, represent mankind as assembled in troops and companies; . . . [a fact which] must be admitted as the foundation of all our reasoning relative to man." [2] There are records of human beings who somehow manage to survive with little care or without normal association with other humans, but such cases of "feral man," as they are called, and of abused and rejected children show few of the characteristics normally attributed to man.[3]

In attempting to account for the apparent regularities of human action and the facts of collective life, sociologists have developed two concepts, *society* and *culture,* which may be considered basic to sociological investigation. Each of these terms has a long history. *Society* derives initially from attempts made during the sixteenth and seventeenth centuries to differentiate the state from the totality of social organization, although systematic analysis of the nature of society came only with the emergence of sociology. The term *culture* gained initial currency in Germany in the eighteenth century, was first used in anthropology by Edward Tylor, an English scholar, in 1871, and has come to be widely used in sociological discourse only in the twentieth century.[4] Both terms have been variously employed, and there is as yet no complete consensus as to their meaning. Despite this variation—or perhaps because of it—they can serve to define and suggest in a general fashion the nature and limits of the subject matter of sociology. It should be noted, however, that the phenomena to which culture and society refer do not exist independently of one another. Although we can distinguish between them analytically, human society cannot exist without culture, and culture exists only within society.

Society

Despite its importance there is no clear-cut agreement as to the meaning of *society*, even among social scientists or, more particularly, sociologists, some of whom have labeled their discipline the "science of society." "In the long history of the literature dealing with the life of human beings in groups," Gladys Bryson has commented, "perhaps no word offers less precision in usage than the word 'society.' " [5] We cannot therefore suggest a definition to which all, or perhaps even most, sociologists would give assent. Nor is there anything to be gained by adding another to the already imposing array of alternatives. Instead we can best carry forward our analysis by exploring the various meanings which have been given to the term and by examining briefly the uses to which they are put. As we pointed out earlier, conceptual differences often mean that people are looking at, or at least emphasizing, different aspects of the same phenomenon.

In its most general usage, society refers merely to the basic fact of human association. For example, the term has been employed

> in the widest sense to include every kind and degree of relationship entered into by men, whether these relations be organized or unorganized, direct or indirect, conscious or unconscious, cooperative or antagonistic. It includes the whole tissue of human relations and is without a boundary or assignable limits. Of amorphous structure itself, it gives rise to numerous, specific, overlapping and interconnected societies, but is not exhausted by them.[6]

This conception of society, which seems on occasion to encompass all of humanity, or mankind at large, serves chiefly to focus our attention upon a broad range of phenomena central to the analysis of human behavior, namely the varied and multiform relationships into which men necessarily enter in the course of group life.

The concept of *social relationship* is based upon the fact that human behavior is oriented in innumerable ways to other persons. Not only do men live together and share common opinions, values, beliefs, and customs, they also continually interact, responding to one another and shaping their behavior in relation to the behavior and expectations of others. The lover's effort to please the object of his affections, the politician's attempts to win the support of the electorate, the soldier's obedience to the orders of his commanding officer—these constitute familiar examples of behavior oriented to the expectations, desires, and wishes, whether real or imagined, of others. Action may be modeled on that of someone else; the child imitates his father, the teen-ager apes her favorite movie star. Behavior may be calculated to elicit responses from others, as in the child's effort to gain parental approval, or the actor's attempt to move his audience. It may be based on expectations as to how others will behave—for example, the boxer's feint before delivering a blow or the doctor's technique in reporting his diagnosis to a patient.

Interaction, however, is not one-sided, as these illustrations may suggest. The electorate responds in some fashion to the politician's actions, and he may then alter his methods or persist in his strategy, with further consequences in the attitudes and behavior of voters. The officer's behavior will be affected by the manner in which his men obey his orders. Courtship is not merely a case of hunter and hunted; to change the metaphor, two can and do play the game as well as one. Interaction, as the word itself suggests, is not a momentary occurrence, not a single response to a single stimulus; it is a persisting process of action and reaction.

A social relationship may be said to exist when individuals or groups possess reciprocal expectations concerning the other's behavior so that they tend to act in relatively patterned ways. To phrase the point differently, a social relationship consists of a pattern of human interaction. Parents and children respond to each other in more or less regular ways, based upon mutual expectations. The patterned interactions of student and teacher, policeman and automobile driver, salesman and buyer, worker and employer, doctor and patient, constitute social relationships of various kinds. From one point of view, then, society is the "web of social relationships."

Society, as the "whole tissue" or "whole complex scheme" of social relationships, can be distinguished from those specific societies in which men group themselves. The emphasis in some definitions of a society, however, is frequently upon the persons rather than upon the structure of relationships. Georg Simmel, one of the founders of modern sociology, considered a society to be "a number of individuals connected by interaction," [7] while the anthropologist Ralph Linton identified a society as "any group of people who have lived and worked together long enough to get themselves organized and to think of themselves as a social unit with well-defined limits." [8] This view of a society, although of value in directing attention to the network of relationships which hold together specific aggregations of people, is too general to be very useful. As thus defined, society could include any of the multiplicity of groups found among men. It could refer to "Society," members of the upper class whose doings are reported in newspaper "society pages." It could encompass organizations of many kinds: the Society of Friends, the Society for the Advancement of Management, the American Ethnological Society, as well as the endless array of clubs, lodges, fraternities, criminal groups, and professional organizations. It could include families, kinship groups, and clusters of friends. Although some writers do use "society" to refer to any kind of group, this term usually denotes a special kind of social unit.

Society, then, is that group within which men can live

a total common life, rather than an organization limited to some specific purpose or purposes. From this point of view a society consists not only of individuals related to one another, but also of interconnected and overlapping groups. Thus, American society comprises 200 million or more individuals (in 1967) tied together in a complex network of relations, of approximately 49 million families (increasing by about .5 million families per year), of the multiplicity of urban and rural communities, religious denominations and sects, political parties, races and ethnic groups, social and economic classes, unions, business and veterans organizations, and the infinite variety of other voluntary organizations into which the population is divided. On the other hand, a simple society such as that of the Andaman Islands west of Burma consisted before the arrival of Europeans of a small population organized primarily into tribes, local groups, and families. The society of India includes the various religious groups, the innumerable castes and the "outcastes," the different races, the many tribes, the economic and political aggregates and organizations, and so on.

In any society smaller groups may be found within larger ones, and individuals simultaneously belong to various groups. Ethnic groups and social classes give rise to voluntary associations, cliques and factions emerge in political parties and other groups, families belong to country clubs and churches and engage in neighborly activities. Each person may participate in a family, a peer group, a business enterprise, or a union or professional organization. A society, then, can be analyzed in terms of its constituent groups and their relations to one another.

Culture

Each society possesses a way of life or, in our terminology, a *culture,* that defines appropriate or required modes of thinking, acting, and feeling. Culture, as thus used in sociological inquiry, has a much wider meaning than it is usually given. In conventional discourse, it refers to the "higher" things in life—painting, music, sculpture, philosophy; the adjective *cultured* stands close to cultivated or refined. In sociology culture refers to the totality of what is learned by individuals as members of society. Taylor's old (1871) but still widely cited definition indicates its scope: "Culture is that complex whole which includes knowledge, belief, art, morals, law, custom, and any other capabilities acquired by man as a member of society." The technique of brushing one's teeth, the Ten Commandments, the rules of baseball or cricket or hop scotch, the procedures for choosing a president or prime minister or members of the Supreme Soviet are as much a part of culture as the latest volume of avantgarde poetry, Beethoven's Ninth Symphony, or the *Analects* of Confucius.

Regularities of behavior do not in themselves constitute culture. They occur in large part because men possess culture, because they have common standards of good and bad, right and wrong, appropriate and inappropriate, and possess similar attitudes and share a fund of knowledge about the environment—social, biological, and physical—in which they live. Culture, George Murdock has noted, is to a large extent "ideational": it refers to the standards, beliefs, and attitudes in terms of which people act.

Recognition of the ubiquity and significance of culture, Ralph Linton has pointed out, is "one of the most important scientific developments of modern times." He continues:

It has been said that the last thing which a dweller in the deep sea would be likely to discover would be water. He would become conscious of its existence only if some accident brought him to the surface and introduced him to air. Man, throughout most of his history, has been only vaguely conscious of the existence of culture and has owed even this consciousness to contrasts between the customs of his own society and those of some other with which he happened to be brought into contact. The ability to see the culture of one's own society as a whole, to evaluate its patterns and appreciate their implications, calls for a degree of objectivity which is rarely if ever achieved.[9]

Because our culture is so much a part of us we take it for granted, frequently assuming that it is a normal, inevitable, and inherent characteristic of all mankind. (The implications of this assumption, known as "ethnocentrism," for the study of society and culture were discussed in Chapter 1.) Anthropologists have often reported that when they ask members of small preliterate groups why they act in some particular fashion they receive an answer which amounts to "That's just the way it's done" or "It's customary." "When Captain Cook asked the chiefs of Tahiti why they ate apart and alone, they simply replied, 'Because it is right.' " [10] Habituated to their own way of life, men frequently can conceive of no other. Among Americans, the expression "It's just human nature" is a characteristic explanation for many actions—competing for fame and power, profit-seeking, marrying for love or for money. Yet this "explanation," which by seemingly explaining everything explains nothing, is itself a manifestation of the ethnocentrism of Americans.

The importance of culture lies in the fact that it provides the knowledge and the techniques that enable man to survive, both physically and socially, and to master and control, insofar as it is possible, the world around him. Man seems to possess few if any instinctive skills and no instinctive knowledge which might enable him to sustain himself, either singly or in groups. The salmon's return from the sea to spawn and die in fresh water, the annual migration of birds from one part of the world to another, the nest-building of the mud wasp, and the complex living patterns of ants and bees are all inherited forms of behavior which seem to appear automatically at the appropriate times.

They are not learned from parents or from other members of the species. Man, on the other hand, survives by virtue of what he learns.

Man is not, however, the only animal that learns to act instead of responding automatically to stimuli. Dogs can be taught a good deal and can learn from experience, as can horses and cats, monkeys and apes, and rats and white mice. But by virtue of his greater brain power and his capacity for language, man can learn more and therefore possesses greater flexibility of action than other animals. He can transmit a great deal of what he learns to others, including his young, and he can in part control the world around him—even to the point of transforming much of it. Man is the only animal to possess culture; indeed, this is one of the crucial distinctions between man and other animals.

Of central importance in the definition of culture is the fact that it is both *learned* and *shared*. Men, we have said, do not inherit their habits and beliefs, their skills and knowledge; they acquire them during the course of their lives. What they learn comes from the groups into which they are born and in which they live. The habits acquired by an infant are likely to be patterned on those of its family and of other persons close at hand. (Not all habits reflect customs or culture, however, for some are merely personal idiosyncrasies.) In an endless number of ways—via explicit instruction, the application of punishment and the offering of rewards, identification with elders and imitation of their behavior—each generation learns from its predecessors. Behavior which is universal, though not learned, or is peculiar to the individual, is not part of culture. (Both unlearned behavior, such as reflexes, and personal idiosyncrasies may, however, be influenced or modified by culture. Indeed, except for biological peculiarities, individual aberrations are defined by their relationship to, or deviation from, cultural patterns.)

The learned and shared character of culture has led

to its occasional identification as the "superorganic" or as man's "social heritage." The former term, used by Herbert Spencer, emphasizes the relative independence of culture from the realm of biology (of which we shall say more in Chapter 3) and its distinctive quality as a product of social life. "Social heritage" calls attention to culture's historical character and therefore to the possibilities of growth and change; it suggests the need for analyzing and understanding its temporal dimensions.

The components of culture

Culture is clearly so inclusive a concept that its principal components should be identified, labeled, analyzed, and related to one another. These components can be grouped roughly in three large categories: institutions, the rules or norms which govern behavior; ideas, that is, knowledge and belief of all varieties—moral, theological, philosophical, scientific, technological, historical, sociological, and so on; and the material products or artifacts which men produce and use in the course of their collective lives.

Institutions

We shall define institutions as *"normative* patterns which define what are felt to be . . . proper, legitimate, or expected modes of action or of social relationship." [11] Such norms or rules pervade all areas of social life: how one eats and what one eats, how one dresses, decorates oneself, responds to others, how one looks after children or the aged, and how one behaves in the presence of members of the opposite sex. Not all behavior conforms to rules, either explicit or implicit, but most actions of any individual reflect the presence of some accepted standards of behavior which he has learned from others and which in some measure he shares with them.

The concept of institution, like that of culture, has been variously defined, and the definition given above, which we shall use, represents only one of several alternatives. Because the other uses of the term appear frequently in sociological literature, it is necessary to detour briefly in order to note these other meanings, even though we shall try to be consistent in our own usage. Earlier definitions, which have been steadily refined or clarified, included not only normative patterns, but also what we shall identify later as groups and as social organization. We still find occasionally in sociological literature (and frequently in everyday discourse) an organized group of individuals referred to as an institution: Harvard College, for example, or the Republican Party. This usage coincides with the early definition by William Graham Sumner: "An institution consists of a concept (idea, notion, doctrine, interest) and a structure. The structure is a framework, or apparatus, or perhaps only a number of functionaries set to cooperate in prescribed ways at a certain conjuncture. The structure holds the concept and furnishes instrumentalities for bringing it into the world of facts and action in a way to serve the interests of men in society." [12] Both the norms *and* the group are included in this definition of an institution. There is an increasing measure of agreement that the term should be used only to refer to patterns of approved or sanctioned behavior, and that other terms should be used to denote the organizational aspects of such behavior and the group of persons involved.

Instead of limiting *institution* to specific social norms or rules—the Ten Commandments, laws against murder or burglary, business practices, or conventions governing daily social intercourse—some writers view an institution as a set of interrelated norms, a "normative system" centered around some type of human activity or some major problem of man in society such as providing subsistence and shelter (property, building techniques, "free enterprise"), caring for children (parenthood, the family), or maintaining order and harmony (the state).[13]

Whether one chooses this encompassing definition or the more limited one used in this volume is largely a semantic problem; there is no inherent correctness in either, and both refer to aspects of social life that are important and require analysis. The definition adopted here provides a generic concept for the variety of norms that govern social behavior: folkway, *mos* (the plural form, *mores,* is conventionally used), custom, convention, fashion, etiquette, law. The definition of *institution* as a "normative system" emphasizes the fact that the multiplicity of rules which govern the actions of men in society are tied together in a more or less organized fashion. There are, however, various ways of identifying (conceptualizing) these systems of norms—as clusters of rules that indicate how persons in particular positions in society, doctors or parents, for example, should act; as bodies of norms that organize the relations of people to one another in social groups; or in terms of their contribution to the performance of socially necessary or important tasks such as educating children or cultivating the soil.

One basic distinction among institutions is that between *folkways* and *mores,* concepts first employed by the pioneer American sociologist William Graham Sumner. A folkway is merely the conventional practice, accepted as appropriate but not insisted upon. The person who does not follow the rule may be looked upon as eccentric or merely as a staunch individualist who refuses to be bound by convention. The occasional man who objects to the irrationality of men's clothing, for example, and refuses under any circumstances to wear a tie is ignoring one of our folkways.

Mores are those norms, or institutions, which are morally strongly sanctioned. Conformity is enforced in various ways, and failure to conform elicits moral disapproval and frequently positive action. Examples are readily available: thou shalt not kill, thou shalt not steal, thou shalt love thy father and mother. Mores are looked upon as essential to the well-being of the group.

The line between folkways and mores is not always easy to draw. Clearly there is a kind of continuum, ranging from those conventions or customs that are loosely observed to those which are most insistently enforced. The rules governing modesty in dress or the consumption of wine and whiskey, for example, may be difficult to categorize. They elicit some moral disapproval if ignored or violated, but clearly do not carry the same moral sanction as adultery, theft, or murder. Moreover, there are wide differences in the attitudes of various social groups toward these rules.

Despite the absence of a sharp dividing line between them, the concepts of folkways and mores possess considerable heuristic value. They focus attention upon significant dimensions or aspects of social norms, the moral sanction attached to them, and the extent to which they are considered to be essential to social well-being.

A second dimension of institutions emerges from the contrast between *customs* and *laws*. The former comprise "long-established usage," those practices that have gradually become accepted as appropriate modes of behavior: the routines of work or leisure, the conventions of warfare, the rituals of religious observance, the etiquette governing social relationships. Customs are sanctioned by tradition and sustained by the pressures of group opinion. Laws, on the other hand, are rules enacted by those who exercise political power and they are enforced through the machinery of the state. They may or may not have the sanction of tradition. They are characteristic of complex societies with well-developed political systems; in those simple societies without distinctive political institutions and recognized sources of political authority law appears, if at all, only in embryonic form. In such simple societies behavior is regulated chiefly by custom, new rules are likely to emerge gradually rather than by formal enactment, and enforcement is not assigned to specific persons operating through a recognized governmental machinery.

The distinction between customs and laws cuts across folkways and mores. Some customs have the moral sanctions characteristic of the mores, while others are more or less casually accepted conventions. Similarly, some laws are supported by strong moral sentiments—thou shalt not kill —while others may virtually lack any moral support, except for whatever attitudes and sentiments sustain conformity with the law in general. Many laws regulating business practice fall into this latter category.

The line between custom and law, like that between folkways and mores, is not always easily drawn, particularly in simpler societies, in which the political structure from which law emerges and through which it is enforced is only partially developed. Even in more complex societies, like our own, the relations between law and custom are frequently complex and distinctions between them difficult to draw. Some customary rules may be embodied in law, Sunday blue laws, for example, whose legal character has sometimes persisted after the customs which gave rise to legislative enactment have changed. Conversely, politically enacted rules may eventually gain an extra-legal, traditional sanction, a process which is clearly apparent in the history of American attitudes toward and sentiments about the Constitution. In addition, laws frequently acquire a barnaclelike accretion of customary practice which is as strongly enforced as though it were written into the law; witness the complex array of conventions and traditional practices governing the actions of Congress.

The concepts of custom and law do not encompass all forms of social norms. There are many institutions that do not seem to fit into either category, despite their apparent inclusiveness. The operating procedures of corporations and the rules of voluntary organizations such as the League of

Women Voters, the National Association of Manufacturers, and the American Medical Association are, with some exceptions, neither sanctioned by tradition nor enforced by the state.

Despite these difficulties the conceptual distinction between law and custom does call attention to important differences in the origins of institutions and in the methods by which they are enforced. There are *crescive* institutions, to use another term drawn from Sumner, which, like Topsy, just grow, and those that are enacted and formally born at a given time. Clearly a different explanation will be required for the origin of a crescive than for an enacted institution, although the latter includes both laws and those formal rules promulgated by officials of nonpolitical organizations. The methods of enforcement may be largely informal, confined to the demands of tradition and the more or less subtly—or obviously—expressed opinions of others, or may be limited to the formal machinery of government, or may, to varying degrees, combine both mechanisms.

These categories for the analysis of institutions do not exhaust the complexity or variety of social norms, or their various aspects or dimensions. For the rules which govern behavior include the transitory standards of fad and fashion, the symbolic rituals of religious and patriotic observance, and the ceremonies which mark significant occasions. They include further the rules of scientific procedure sanctioned neither by tradition nor by legislative enactment, but only by the rationally based consensus of scientists and the empirically tested methods of rational economic enterprise, although all these rational norms may, of course, contain traditional or customary elements.

Institutions, we have said, account, in their many forms, for much of the regularity of behavior that we observe; it is because men possess these learned and shared standards that their actions seem to be alike, or at least similar. This statement, however, may suggest a degree of conformity that typically does not exist. Norms vary in the degree of conformity that they require, depending in some measure upon the nature of the approved or interdicted behavior. One cannot be just a little bit of a murderer. On the other hand, the amount of time which college students may be expected, or required, to devote to their studies may vary widely. The rules of dress, etiquette, and speech may be couched in such general terms that some variety will be expected within the limits set by the culture. In many cases, that is to say, the norms prescribe a range of behavior or set the limits beyond which it would be inappropriate or wrong to stray.

Even when the institution is precisely defined, the actual behavior of men and women is likely to vary around the norm from virtual nonconformity to elaborate overconformity. In many colleges and universities, for example, students are expected to devote two hours to study for each hour spent in class, or about thirty hours each week for a student carrying fifteen hours of class work. It is probably safe to say that most students do not meet this requirement; the actual time spent may vary from none to forty or fifty or even sixty hours per week, with an average probably somewhat less than thirty. Any analysis of institutions and behavior and the relations obtaining between them must therefore take into account the fact that both the definition of social norms and the description of actual conduct often refer to a range of behavior around some central tendency.

It is, of course, obvious that many institutions are often ignored in practice, that men break the Ten Commandments, do not give their seats to women in public conveyances, and doctor their income-tax returns. They defy the sex mores, disregard conventions governing work and play, and ignore the requirements of fashion. Indeed, the starting place for much sociological inquiry has been the effort to account for socially deviant activities—crime, delinquency, divorce, suicide—rather than for conventional behavior.

The fact that men do ignore or violate social norms indicates that conformity too cannot be taken for granted and must also be explained. When one accounts for patterned behavior by reference to cultural definitions of proper or expected behavior, one has taken only the first step in sociological analysis. Institutions are not self-enforcing, and it is necessary to discover why men conform to social rules, as well as ascertaining how institutions arise and what circumstances account for their persistence and for the changes that take place in them. In part, of course, men conform to social norms because they are taught to do so; they learn the customs and conventions of their culture as they are brought up and educated (see the discussion of *socialization,* Chapter 4). In part, they conform because of sanctions, pressures, and controls which are institutionalized and built into the structure of society.

Ideas: Beliefs, Knowledge, and Values

The second major component of culture, *ideas,* encompasses a varied and complex array of social phenomena. It includes the beliefs men hold about themselves and the social, biological, and physical world in which they live, and about their relations to one another, to society and nature, and to such other beings and forces as they may discover, accept, or conjure up. It embraces the whole vast body of ideas by which men account for their observation and experience—folklore, legends, proverbs, theology, science, philosophy, practical know-how—and which they take into account or rely upon in choosing alternative lines of action. It encompasses the forms in which men express their feelings about themselves and others and their responses, emotional and aesthetic, to the world around them.

In addition to cognitive and expressive ideas, men also learn and share the values by which they live, the standards and ideals by which they define their goals, select a course of action, and judge themselves and others: success, rationality, honor, courage, patriotism, loyalty, efficiency. These values are not specific rules for action but general precepts to which men give their allegiance and about which they are likely to have strong feelings. They represent as well the shared attitudes of approval and disapproval, the judgments of good or bad, desirable or undesirable, toward specific persons, things, situations, and events.

The term *value,* however, is sometimes used for the *objects* or *situations* which are defined as good, proper, desirable, worthwhile: for money, wives, jewelry, success, power, fame, rather than for shared sentiments or judgments. Values then acquire their character by virtue of men's judgments but are distinguished from them. It is this distinction that Robert M. MacIver emphasizes in differentiating between attitudes and interests, between the "*subjective* reactions, states of consciousness within the individual human being, with relation to *objects*" and the objects themselves.[14] Values, as things to which men assign desirability or importance, may then be beliefs or institutions, as well as the third general component of culture, material objects. The views men express as to the nature of God, or of man or society itself, may be subscribed to so intensely that they become objects of value; men may possess as strong an interest in their belief in God or their commitment to some scientific doctrine as they do in money or power. "For a vested interest in understanding," John K. Galbraith writes, "is more preciously guarded than any other treasure." [15] Similarly, institutions acquire value in men's eyes, and certainly many of the material objects created by men become the locus of approval or disapproval, desire or envy.

That men should evaluate their property, their laws and customs, ideas, and even themselves and others is perhaps inevitable as they make the choices inherent in social life.

Viewing the same phenomenon from different conceptual perspectives—as instruments of production, rules governing behavior, or beliefs orienting man to nature and society, on the one hand, and as objects of value on the other—is not necessarily a source of confusion; it is rather a means for widening our vision and increasing our understanding.

The ideas men share—cognitive, expressive, and evaluative—consist of a body of symbols through which they can communicate with one another. Communication is a fundamental social process, for it is only through the exchange of ideas that organized social life is possible. What distinguishes man from other creatures is the development of a symbolic language that goes beyond crude signs or signals which can convey only limited information or serve as direct stimuli to action. While other animals communicate through gestures and a relatively simple assortment of sounds, only man has evolved a language which can express abstract ideas and the complexities of emotional or aesthetic response. As the philosopher Ernst Cassirer has pointed out, what transformed Helen Keller from a blind deaf-mute capable only of very limited participation in social life into a fully human being was the flash of insight that words stood for things, that "everything has a name." [16] Symbolic language is both a basic constituent of culture and that which makes its elaboration and cumulation possible.

Some writers would confine the term *culture* only to the body of ideas, the symbols that men share and through which they exchange meaningful communication, thus distinguishing it from the system or structure of social relationships. This definition can be very useful and appears to be gaining substantial currency among sociologists. It enables one to distinguish between symbolic systems—language, beliefs, knowledge, and expressive forms—and their interrelations in contrast to the organized pattern of interaction among individuals and groups.[17]

Material Culture

The third major component of culture is perhaps the easiest to define. It consists of those material things that men create and use, ranging from the primitive instruments of prehistoric man to the most advanced machinery of modern man. It includes the stone ax and the electronic computer, the outrigger canoe of the Polynesians and the luxury liner, the teepee of the Indians and the skyscraper of the modern city.

To identify these material objects as elements of culture without reference to their nonmaterial concomitants, however, can easily be misleading. When we refer to such objects we are apt to take for granted their uses, their value, and the requisite practical or theoretical know-how. Yet machines or tools obviously are hardly useful unless their owners possess the knowledge and skill needed to operate or apply them. The same objects may be put to many alternative uses. Rings, for example, may be worn on one's fingers, arms, or legs, or may be put through one's lips, nose, or ears; all these uses may be found among the peoples of the world. The Quonset huts so familiar to World War II veterans as barracks or office quarters have been subsequently used as homes, garages, storage buildings, barns, factories, and roadside hot-dog stands. In William Morris's Utopian novel, *News from Nowhere,* the Houses of Parliament are reduced to storage houses for dung.

With different uses, of course, go different evaluations and meanings. Paintings may be treasured and displayed or hidden in the attic, seen as great artistic achievements or the scribblings of eccentrics. Automobiles may be visible symbols of social standing or merely practical utilities which provide transportation. Two crossed pieces of wood may be a religious symbol or fuel to be burned in order to keep warm. The division between ideas—knowledge, values, traditional beliefs—and material culture, though often useful, is therefore in a sense quite arbitrary, for to describe cultural artifacts fully it is necessary to know their uses, the attitudes taken toward them, and the body of knowledge and skills needed to produce them.

The organization of culture

It has been necessary, in this description of the components of culture, to refer several times to the complex relationships which exist among the several elements that make up the whole, between institutions and values, for example, or between values and artifacts. These relationships constitute one significant focus of sociological analysis. This analysis may remain at the level of culture in general, or, more frequently, it can be directed toward *a* culture, the cluster or system of institutions, values, beliefs, and objects possessed by a particular group of people. Thus we may consider separately American culture, the culture of India, of the Trobriand Islanders of the Western Pacific, and of the many separate tribes, peoples, and nations of the world. It is only by comparing these specific cultures that we may eventually enlarge our understanding of culture in general.

The components of any particular culture are not randomly assorted, but form a more or less coherent whole. Institutions such as marriage, for example, must be seen in relation to the values that men and women pursue in family life, norms governing the division of labor, and the general values concerning the place of men and women and the rights of individuals. The structure of the culture—its organizing principles and the relations among the parts— is therefore relevant to an understanding of any specific cultural pattern.

The components of any culture, as well as the culture as a whole, can be thought of as consisting of more or less independent systems, each with its own structure or organization. There is in the mores, Sumner pointed out, "a strain toward consistency," and a similar tendency is to be found throughout the culture and within its components —institutions, values, expressive symbols, bodies of knowledge, technological systems. There is nothing automatic about these tendencies; they emerge because men characteristically try to reduce the tension or conflict generated by contradictory or competing demands or ideas, and to maintain some order in their relations with one another.

Role and status

By establishing rules that govern behavior and values by which men judge their own actions and those of others, culture also defines the pattern of social interaction that binds men together in an organized social life. Of central importance in analyzing social interaction are the concepts of *role* and *status*. These concepts provide a link between the analysis of *society* and of *culture,* and are of considerable value in establishing the relationships between the individual and his culture and society. (We shall have more to say of this problem in Chapter 4.)

The concepts of role and status derive from certain basic observations about the nature of institutions. As one considers the variety of social norms or standards of behavior it is apparent that relatively few of them apply universally to all people. Some apply only to limited groups, others only to one person. Some apply in one context in which an individual happens to be; others apply in different contexts. We find these points illustrated by one of our basic and presumably universal mores: thou shalt not kill. The person who commits murder is guilty of the most serious crime in the whole criminal calendar. If caught he may be subject to the extreme penalty, or at least to the maximum possible penalty. But this rule does not apply

to certain people under specified circumstances. The policeman in pursuit of his duty, the public executioner carrying
out the edict of a legally constituted court, the soldier in
battle, even on occasion the husband betrayed—these may
kill another person or persons without being subject to
criticism or sanction. Nor do we define such killings as
murder; our verbal distinctions reveal our social values.
The central fact in these illustrations is that the rule does
not apply to people who occupy certain *positions* in society.
The terms used in our illustrations—policeman, public
executioner, soldier, husband—refer to such positions, or,
in sociological terms, *statuses.* Each of these statuses carries
with it a set of rules or norms which prescribe how the
person who occupies it should or should not behave under
particular circumstances. That cluster of norms we call a
role. Status and role are thus two sides of a single coin.
Status is a socially identified position; role is the pattern
of behavior expected or required of persons who occupy
a particular status.

The concept of role is, of course, not new, as illustrated
by Shakespeare's oft-quoted lines:

> All the world's a stage,
> And all the men and women merely players:
> They have their exits and their entrances;
> And one man in his time plays many parts,
> His acts being seven ages.

These ages or, to use our modern and less poetic vocabulary,
roles, included the infant, schoolboy, lover, soldier, "justice,"
"pantaloon," and lastly "second childishness."

The long ancestry of the idea of social role does not
necessarily mean, however, that the concept has been systematically used in the past. One will frequently find that some
concept can be traced back to Biblical or classical sources,
or to the writings of philosophers or poets or novelists. Our

earlier citations of Aristotle and of Adam Ferguson give evidence that many basic ideas have been available for a very long time, a fact that has sometimes given rise to the argument that sociology frequently offers nothing more than familiar knowledge in a new package. What is new about the concept of role, or of many other modern concepts which embody older ideas, is the attempt to organize knowledge systematically, to test ideas against an accumulation of evidence, and to further knowledge by pushing beyond the original perceptions. The atomic theory of matter, it has been pointed out, probably was first formulated by Democritus, but the ancient Greeks possessed no science of physics which enabled them to split the atom. That men play "many parts" is familiar, but the systematic analysis of the relations among them, the processes by which they are acquired and learned, the "strains" that may exist among the roles one plays, and the relationships between roles and personality provide fresh insight into behavior. Science consists not merely of acute and penetrating observations (as the social sciences are sometimes viewed) but of orderly and cumulative development of knowledge. It entails the integration of findings so that they do not remain the random perceptions of wise men, sometimes erroneous and sometimes only partly true, but become firmly established scientific lore available to all.

Nonetheless we can use Shakespeare's theatrical image to develop and explain the concepts of role and status. Theatrical roles performed by "players" exist independently of the individuals, who must learn their lines and acquire the appropriate gestures and manners. Social roles are also learned as men and women acquire the culture of their group, although roles may become so much a part of the individual personality that they are played without awareness of their social character. (It is interesting to note that professional actors have long argued about the extent to which they must "live" their parts in order to perform them well.[18]) Roles are not people; they are the parts played on the social stage, and they can be analyzed separately just as the drama can be considered apart from the performance and the performers.

The elements of a social role are both obvious and subtle. We know, for example, what a teacher is supposed to do in his professional role: to transmit to his students some kind of information or skill, and to follow more or less acceptable and understood methods of doing so. But in some communities a teacher also has been expected to avoid tobacco and liquor, and female teachers are not expected to wear slacks in public. In a study of the sex roles of college women it was reported that many of them "played dumb," belittled their intellectual achievements, and submitted to male leadership and authority when on dates because they felt that this was what men expected of them.[19] In an investigation of local union leadership in the United Automobile Workers it was discovered that union officers were expected to give no evidence of personal ambition. "The worst that can be said of a union leader is that he is an 'opportunist,' or that he is 'ambitious.' "[20]

As these illustrations suggest, many features of a social role are only implicit. As social actors men become aware of some of the rules which govern their behavior only when others disregard them or when the question of ignoring or violating them comes up. An important task of sociology is to discover not only the obvious and explicit norms which define and regulate men's actions but also those which usually remain hidden beneath the surface.

Men can be said to play or perform social roles; they fill or occupy statuses. Status is a kind of social identification tag which places people in relation to others and which also always implies some kind of role. Each man occupies many statuses and plays many roles. A man is a husband or bachelor or widower, a business executive or factory worker or professional, a Catholic or Protestant or Jew. He is a community leader or an ordinary citizen, a baseball fan, an avid fisherman, an amateur photographer. Each of these identifications constitutes a status and carries with it expectations of behavior, however precisely or vaguely defined, however rigidly or loosely enforced.

How a person behaves, therefore, depends in large part upon the particular position in which he finds himself—or in which he would like to be—and the role expectations that go with it. For example, a teacher is expected to disregard the sex of his students in assigning or evaluating their academic work. (The occasional teacher-student marriage indicates that sometimes the teacher has failed to ignore the sex of at least one of his students or, more likely, that teacher and student have encountered one another outside the classroom where they could disregard their academic roles and behave as male and female—although these are also socially defined roles and not merely biologically shaped patterns of behavior.) The tightfisted businessman who is very generous in his contributions to charity and the hard-boiled racketeer who treats his wife, children, and aged mother with love and affection are not necessarily illustrative of hypocrisy or split personality, nor is the Indian warrior who carefully protected his loved ones by joyfully removing the scalps of his enemies. They are all behaving at different times in ways appropriate to the particular statuses they happen to be occupying and the roles they are playing. When a man refuses to raise the wages of his employees or sets out ruthlessly to take business away from his competitor, perhaps even to drive him out of business, he is acting as a businessman; in responding to an appeal from some charity he is behaving as a respected and influential member of the local community. The racketeer may shed his "business" role when he crosses his threshold in the evening.

The importance of social roles lies not only in the extent to which they regulate behavior, but also in the fact

that they enable men to predict the actions of others and
therefore to fashion their own actions accordingly. Social
relationships therefore exist between or among the roles
played by members of a society. These relationships are
not only indirectly defined by values which provide general
standards of behavior—courtesy, respect, obedience—but
also by specific institutional prescriptions which indicate
how occupants of defined statuses are expected to behave
toward one another. Judges are not supposed to give preference to a litigant in a court on the basis of his age, sex,
religion, wealth, or color (unless such preference is legally
defined). Children are expected to follow their parents'
rules as to when they go to bed, whether or not they can
go out to play, and what they should eat for dinner. Men
should tip their hats to women, walk on the outside of the
sidewalk when accompanying women, and rise when a
woman enters the room.

As our illustrations may suggest, roles and statuses are
built upon various kinds of foundations. Certain biological
facts provide the basis for differentiating some roles and
statuses. In every society different roles are built upon the
facts of age and sex. We distinguish, for example, infant,
child, adolescent, adults of different varieties—young adults,
the middle-aged, the old. In every society men and women
occupy distinct positions and are expected to behave differently, even to vary in character and personality, although
societies differ widely in their definitions of sexual roles.
Other biological features are sometimes, though not universally, seized upon as the basis for distinct statuses and
roles. In Western society, as Talcott Parsons has shown in
some detail, the ill person occupies a definite position which
permits, encourages, and even requires certain kinds of
behavior.[21]

But most roles and statuses emerge from the process
of collective living itself. There is always some economic

division of labor which entails the differentiation of positions and duties. As men deal with problems of maintaining order and harmony in society there develop distinct political roles and statuses: congressman, M.P., commissar, mayor, party chairman, precinct captain, judge. Religious practices and beliefs provide other grounds for social differentiation: priest, monk, nun, bishop, minister, deacon, rabbi. As societies grow larger and more complex, new positions and new expectations of behavior emerge: movie star, astronaut, probation officer, nursery school teacher, computer programmer, propagandist, atomic physicist, go-fors (errand boys for theatrical producers and directors), beatniks, *tummlers* (social directors in Catskill Mountain resorts—"a versatile *jongleur,* who performed frenetically around the clock and twice as fast on rainy days to keep restive guests from checking out" [22]), and countless others.

Among the many statuses men may come to occupy, we may distinguish those which are *ascribed* and those which are *achieved*. An ascribed status derives from attributes over which a person has no control—age, sex, or color, for example—or from membership in a group to which he is assigned by others—family, religion, nationality. On the basis of an ascribed status he is expected to acquire and perform certain roles. An achieved status is entered upon by some direct or positive action: One must get married in order to become a husband or wife, secure a majority of votes cast to become a Congressman, or graduate from medical school in order to become a doctor. Ascription limits access to status positions: A man cannot become a woman, a Boston Irishman cannot become a Lowell or Cabot, an Indian untouchable can never be a member of the Brahmin caste. Insofar as the number of persons who can fill a particular status is restricted—only a limited number of students are admitted to medical school, only one person at a time can be President, not everyone can rise to the top in industry—potential occupants must compete, demonstrating in some fashion their abilities to perform the relevant role.

One of the more significant aspects of a status is the value placed upon it, the respect or prestige it carries in the eyes of others. Each position—and its correlative role—is ranked by members of a society as superior or inferior. Doctors in the United States, to take an obvious example, have a higher social standing than pharmacists, and tool-makers rank higher than farm laborers. In many societies warriors have been more highly esteemed than merchants or artisans. Thus Herodotus, the ancient Greek historian, observed: "The Thracians, the Scyths, the Persians, the Lydians, and almost all other barbarians, hold the citizens who practice trades, and their children, in less repute than the rest, while they esteem as noble those who are aloof from handicrafts, and especially honour such as are given wholly to war." In classical China, on the other hand, warriors were ranked below scholars.

Status is used frequently to refer only to the ranking of a social position or role, or of the occupants of such roles, and one major aspect of any society is the hierarchy of roles and of persons, which constitutes one aspect of its organiza-tion or structure. This ranking is sociologically important because it contributes to the ordering of social interaction and the structure of social relationships and provides moti-vation for various kinds of social behavior; the by now familiar term "status-seeking" refers to behavior designed to enhance one's social standing or lead to the acquisition of a more prestigious social position.

Groups, categories, and statistical aggregates

The complex array of roles and statuses that define the behavior of individuals and their relations with one another constitutes what sociologists call *social organization* or *social structure*. The term *social structure* is used occasionally to refer to any patterned regularity of behavior or interaction. This latter use emphasizes the element of pattern in the term "structure," but we shall stress the element of relationship among parts implicit in the word.

Social organization, however, also contains a variety of interconnected and often overlapping groups or collectivities, each with its own particular structure of roles and statuses. In everyday conversation, *group* is usually applied indiscriminately to many different collections of people. A handful of mountaineers operating an illicit still in the Kentucky hills, members of a ladies' club, a teen-age gang in Harlem or the Bronx, a Boy Scout troop, the 60,000 or so workers at the Ford River Rouge plant, the more than a million members of the United Automobile Workers, and the employees of U.S. Steel are all likely to be called "groups." So are the President's Cabinet, the some 100,000 people who each year attend the Army–Navy football game, and the mob of irate southerners who surrounded Little Rock High School when Negro students first tried to enter its doors in September, 1957. Each nation is frequently identified as a group, as are the innumerable families, clans, moieties, and tribes found among primitive peoples. Members of the Catholic Church, Jews, government employees, a movie audience, beatniks, the rich and the poor, those earning from $4,000 to $5,000 a year, members of the Democratic or Republican Party, the Communist Party of the Soviet Union, professors, electricians, bankers, men, women, fans of some popular singer or movie actress, readers of comic books or of sociology texts—each of these is likely to be labeled in ordinary conversation as a group. Within some of these "groups" there may be still others: The Catholic Church is divided into parishes and dioceses, into a number of religious orders such as the Dominicans, Franciscans, and Jesuits; it contains such distinct entities as the college of Cardinals and the Curia Romana (the papal administration). Within the government bureaucracy are the innumerable offices, bureaus, agencies, departments, and interdepartmental committees, as well as informal cliques and sets of friends. Political parties have their national and state committees, precinct organizations, and factions; labor unions have locals, departments, and executive committees.

This legion of groups is obviously so diversified that it would be difficult, if not impossible, to characterize them in general terms. A family, with its relatively limited numbers, its recognized roles and statuses, and its sense of corporate identity clearly differs in important ways from the Catholic Church, with its elaborate hierarchical organization and its millions of members who share a set of beliefs and values and follow the same religious practices; from electricians or bankers who possess the same status but have little if any awareness of a collective identity; and from admirers of a popular singer who are grouped together simply because they share a single attribute. Sociologists therefore face the task of distinguishing types of human collectivities and establishing a precise language for their analysis.

As a first step in performing this task we may distinguish among social groups, social categories, and statistical aggregates.

A social group consists of a number of persons whose relationships are based upon a set of interrelated roles and statuses. They interact with one another in a more or less standardized fashion determined largely by the norms and values they accept. They are united or held together by a sense of common identity or a similarity of interests which enables them to differentiate members from nonmembers. The social group then is identified by three attributes: patterned interaction, shared or similar beliefs and values, and, to use Franklin H. Giddings' phrase, consciousness of kind.

In defining a social group in this way we have narrowed the meaning conventionally assigned to it, limiting its reference and making it somewhat more precise. A family, according to this definition, is a group, as is a labor union, a social club, a number of friends who see one another occasionally, and the students of a college or university. Men, women, owners of television sets, adolescents, hoboes, and readers of *True Story* magazine are not social groups.

These collections of people who do not possess the attributes of a group can be separated in turn into two distinct divisions. One, which we may call a *social category*, consists of persons who have a similar status and therefore in this respect perform the same social role—for instance, men, electricians, adolescents, bankers, or hoboes. The second, which we call a *statistical aggregate*, is made up of persons who possess a similar social attribute by virtue of which they can logically be thought of together—the readers of comic books and readers of *Harper's Magazine*, addicts of rock and roll and admirers of Brigitte Bardot, baseball fans, jazz devotees, and persons who commit suicide.

Although sociologists are chiefly concerned with social groups and categories, statistical aggregates are also, inevitably, important subjects for analysis. Often we wish to explain why people fall into particular aggregates, or to account for the differences between them. Why do some people read *Harper's Magazine* while others read *True Story*? Why do some Englishmen read the pontifical London *Times* while others read the tabloid *Daily Express*? Who are the readers of detective stories, the admirers of rock and roll, the people who commit suicide, and those who become drug addicts? In answering these questions, structural facts —that is, some information about the groups to which men belong and the statuses they occupy—will usually be necessary. Protestants commit suicide more often than Catholics, readers of *Harper's* are more likely to be professionals than readers of *True Story,* adolescents are more likely to prefer rock and roll than are adults. These facts provide the beginning of explanations which require some further knowledge of the nature of the groups people come from and of the roles they play.

Statistical aggregates are also important because they sometimes point to significant aspects of social structure or provide the basis for the emergence of social groups. A common interest in baseball, for example, or in modern jazz or antiques may be one of the ties that bind a group of friends together. Respect for physical prowess may be the basis upon which teen-age gangs select their leaders. An income of more than $10,000 per year may enable its recipients to achieve positions of high reputability in the community. In some cases, persons with similar attributes coalesce into groups: Fans of a popular singer become a mob trying to tear the shirt off his back or, more quietly, join fan clubs; rabid racists establish Citizens' Councils, or ride out in white sheets to terrorize Negroes; admirers of George Bernard Shaw establish Shavian societies.

Social categories share with statistical aggregates potentialities for the emergence of full-fledged groups. Because of this fact Morris Ginsberg has lumped together as *quasigroups*

> such entities as social classes, which, without being groups, are a recruiting field for groups, and whose members have certain characteristic modes of behavior in common; and other incipient groups such as collections of individuals interested in the same pursuits or favouring the same policy, for example, employers of labour who have not yet formed any association in the defense of their interests, or individuals interested in particular sports, or in social reform, who yet possess no definite organization.[23]

By virtue of their common physical attributes, Negroes, for example, can be classified as a statistical aggregate. To the extent that they are assigned a particular status in society they become a social category. Because of the difficulties caused by their position they have tended to become "race conscious," to form voluntary organizations to improve their circumstances. They seek to eliminate discrimination and constraints imposed upon them because they are Negroes and to achieve the status their individual abilities warrant. Some wish racial attributes to be reduced merely to characteristics of a statistical aggregate, whereas others try to establish a distinctive culture and social identity as the basis for a cohesive social group.

One task of the sociologist is to specify the conditions under which the transformation from category or aggregate to group takes place. What forces, for example, lead a social class to become conscious of its existence and problems and to act as a more or less cohesive whole? When do workers form unions, employers an employers' association, or consumers a league for the protection of their interests? Why do movie fans join clubs and professional men join civic associations and professional societies?

The concepts of group, category, and statistical aggregate are sometimes difficult to apply to specific collections of people. Although many human aggregations are readily subsumed under one or another of these concepts, others are ambiguous in character and defy ready classification. From one point of view American physicians are merely a social category, from another they constitute a highly organized and powerful association. Many members of a social class have little sense of a collective identity, but others may be strongly "class-conscious" and seek to develop class-based organizations. Advocates of a proposed reform may be in process of establishing a new political group, and members of an emerging profession may be hesitantly feeling their way toward formation of a professional society.

These concepts, then, serve chiefly as heuristic devices, that is, they suggest questions and direct inquiry. Discussion in general terms of groups, social categories, and statistical aggregates takes us but a short step in the direction of systematic analysis. Merely determining that a particular collection of people is one or the other provides only a minimal beginning for systematic study; after this determination has been made one must proceed to account for the existence of a statistical aggregate, or explore the nature of a particular category and its significance for society, or analyze the structure and functions of a social group.

The definition of a social group is also essentially of heuristic value: It calls attention to significant variables which must be examined. Interaction, values, solidarity, the defining characteristics of social groups, are, after all, variable; they do not possess a fixed "value," if we may borrow mathematical terminology. There may be more or less interaction among persons who stand to one another in diverse kinds of relationships. Members of a group may subscribe to only one norm or belief or many, or may hold to their ideas with differing degrees of intensity. Members may be strongly or weakly identified with each other; the group, that is, may be more or less solidary. Each of these variables must then be examined and its relationship to others determined.

Types of social groups

The distinction between social groups, social categories, and statistical aggregates, we have said, is only a first step toward the ordering and classification of human collectivities. The enormous variety of social groups, a variety that we clearly recognize in our everyday vocabulary with such terms as *crowd, audience, public, clique, gang, club, fraternity, association,* has led to many attempts to establish a taxonomy of groups similar to that used in biology to classify plants and animals. Theoretically, any such classification must rest upon an explicit principle (the *fundamentum divisionis*) that should have a significant relationship to other facts of social life; to divide men into those with red hair and those without, for example, may make logical or aesthetic sense, but it is not likely to lead to any sociological understanding. Many criteria have been used in the classification of social groups, both those which we have already identified as the variables that define the group and other group attributes such as size, duration, function, and location. Unfortunately, none of these all-encompassing efforts has been very helpful in analysis and research. Sociologists therefore continue to employ categories based upon diverse criteria to describe and analyze various kinds of groups. Although these categories do not meet the criteria of a logical taxonomy—they are not mutually exclusive nor do they encompass all the groups with which we are familiar—they identify the more important kinds of social groups.

Perhaps the central problem in the analysis of groups is the nature of the relations existing among their members. One fundamental distinction is between those groups characterized by close and intimate relations, the *primary group,* and those that lack such relations. The primary group includes the play group, friends, family, in some cases the neighborhood, and even on occasion an entire, necessarily small, society. Relations within a primary group tend to be personal, permissive of spontaneity, and typically (although not necessarily) long-lasting; they are based upon diffuse, generalized mutual expectations rather than upon narrowly defined and precise obligations. Members of a family are expected to love one another, while workers in an office associate with one another only in ways required by their jobs—unless they become friendly, that is, develop a *primary* relationship. The members of a primary group are held together by the intrinsic value of the relations themselves rather than by a commitment to an explicit organizational goal.

The family, although clearly a primary group, occupies a special category. Unlike more spontaneous and informally based groups, its existence is institutionally sanctioned. It is based to some degree on biological facts of sex and age, but its structure is defined by law and tradition. Everyone belongs to a family and familial roles are more or less the same for all family groups within a society or a culturally distinct segment within it.

In contrast with the primary group, *associations* are made up of individuals who come together to seek some common goal or goals, or in advocacy of a like or common interest. Although primary groups and relations characteristically develop within such "secondary" groups as trade unions, business corporations, governmental agencies, political parties, schools and universities, farmers' cooperatives, and fraternal societies, these associations are typically organized in a *formal* or *bureaucratic* fashion. Relations among members tend to be formal and impersonal, clearly formulated rules govern much of the behavior of members, and possibilities of spontaneity are limited. Roles tend to be segmental, that is, limited in their requirements to the official or formal tasks performed as members of the group, rather than inclusive. A familiar example of formal organization can be seen in the modern office, with its allocation of duties to secretaries, typists, clerks, office manager, receptionist, telephone operator, and others, with clear lines of authority and responsibility, and with the entire functioning of the office governed by a more or less explicit set of rules and regulations, frequently set down in some kind of rule book.

In addition to these two types of organization—the primary group and the formal association—there are other significant kinds of social groupings that must be included in any analysis of the structure of society. *Ethnic groups* are made up of persons who share a common cultural tradition which unites them in a single social entity. From one point of view, any society, with its distinctive culture, constitutes an ethnic group. But within many of the politically unified societies of the modern world some groups are set off to some degree by their practices, beliefs, religion, or language—and in some cases by distinctive physical characteristics as well. In the United States there are the Irish, Italians, Japanese, Chinese, Mexicans, French-Canadians, Jews, Greeks, Indians, and so on. In Belgium there are the Walloons and the Flemish; in Switzerland the German-, French-, Italian-, and Romansh-speaking groups; in the Union of South Africa the Afrikaaners, English, Jews, Cape Colored, and the Blacks (the latter divided into many distinct tribes); in the Soviet Union the Great Russians, Ukrainians, Latvians, Lithuanians, Jews, Uzbeks, Georgians, and several dozen more.

Membership in an ethnic group is ascribed; individuals derive their ethnic status from the family into which they are born and acquire its cultural attributes as they grow up. Sharing a cultural tradition that in some measure marks them off, members of an ethnic group are likely to associate more frequently among themselves than with outsiders and to share a common identity that in turn affects their relations to one another and to others. The clarity with which an ethnic group can be distinguished, the degree to which its members hang together, and the extent of their loyalty to the group of course vary widely. Moreover, the internal structure of the group is significantly affected by its position in the larger society, that is, its relations to other groups.

Ethnic differences are frequently closely tied to *social classes,* groups that are arranged in some order of superiority or inferiority in society. Although sometimes ill-defined, social classes play an important part in any society. Classes are sometimes identified as groups, sometimes as social categories; in fact they may be either. Some students identify classes by economic position, others by social standing or rank in the community, still others by political power. We need not deal here with the complex problems raised by these diverse approaches; all of these structural divisions are important in the life of a society, and they are typically closely related to one another.

Members of a class share a common position—economic, social, or political—that may be ascribed or achieved. A person acquires his class position initially from his family; indeed, families rather than individuals constitute the units of social class. Even in the United States, where the ideology of "equal opportunity" dominates and status is presumably based chiefly upon achievement, there are obvious advantages in being the son of a rich and well-known man rather than of a poor one. Other societies—India, for example—give much less room for achievement and rely much more heavily upon ascription to place people in the social order.

A common class position is likely to carry with it similar values, beliefs, and ways of acting—although there may well be differences in behavior and attitude between persons born into a class and those who move into it by their own efforts—or lack of effort. These common characteristics may lead to a corporate awareness or class consciousness that binds members into a social unit and propels leaders to collective action. One problem for sociologists, as we noted earlier, is to identify the conditions under which the shift from a social category to a group occurs and to assess the consequences.

Primary groups, associations, ethnic groups, and social classes are obviously not mutually exclusive and their complex interrelationships constitute a central problem in the analysis of social organization. The ubiquitous primary group is found within associations, ethnic groups, and classes. Associations are sometimes organized by primary groups seeking to achieve a specific goal, and some primary groups will in all likelihood be found within most associations, even the most bureaucratic. Since members of ethnic groups, by virtue of their common culture, and of classes, because of their similar economic or social position, are likely to be thrown together frequently, they typically give rise to a multitude of primary groups which may play a significant role in the organized life of these larger groups.

Classes and ethnic groups provide a "recruiting field," in Ginsberg's phrase, for the emergence of associations. The existence of associations limited to members of one class or ethnic group may be merely a matter of happenstance; they may be confined to one group merely because the members live close together or are thrown into frequent and regular contact. A businessmen's club in a predominantly Irish or Jewish section of a large city, for example, is obviously likely to be confined to members of one ethnic group, even if they are not drawn together by ethnic interests. Their ethnic character, however, may then affect the aims and activities of the organization. Class and ethnic associations may, on the other hand, represent group efforts to protect themselves or to advance their common interests, as in the case of trade unions, or any of the many organizations formed by the numerous ethnic groups in the United States.

Relations between classes and ethnic groups are often complex, for they substantially affect one another. Discrimination against a particular ethnic group may largely determine its class position; the majority of American Negroes are confined to poorly paid manual or service occupations. Exclusion from opportunities for education or from desirable occupations for racial or ethnic reasons confines members to a low class position. On the other hand, an entire group's class position affects the way in which it is treated by the rest of the society. Collective action as well as personal interaction among members of different groups may then be based on a complex intermingling of both ethnic and class interests and attitudes.

The groups we have thus far examined function within a larger territorially defined whole in which men pursue their various activities. This large, inclusive group, when defined in territorial terms, is the *community*. Unlike other groups, it is defined in part by its physical location, which also provides a significant bond of solidarity.

There is an obvious overlap between community and society, and in small cohesive societies they are virtually identical. But within most societies there are usually the geographically distinguished subdivisions which we call towns, villages, hamlets, cities, and, sometimes, neighborhoods within cities. As parts of a larger whole these communities are usually not independent, yet it is possible for men to live out their lives within their borders. Even in the metropolis one finds areas in which many local residents were born and reared, in which they work, find their leisure, marry, have families, and expect to be buried.[24]

In describing and analyzing the community one necessarily examines the diverse groups which take form within it and their relations to one another. One considers the relations of the community to other communities and to the larger whole of which it is a part. But there are also distinctive qualities of the community as such that affect the groups within it, their relations to one another and to the whole. In such conventional terms as *urban, rural, small town,* and *suburban* we obviously recognize the existence of overall differences which warrant close inspection. Some of these differences are readily apparent: sheer size and number, the physical concentration or dispersion of the population, and characteristic occupations. Others—in modes of communication, values, and styles of life, for example—are more subtle and complex, though they have far-reaching cultural and structural consequences.

Types of societies

As one considers the diverse groups and the complex combinations and interrelationships to be found among them, one is likely to ask whether it is possible to sort out some overall pattern of social organization characteristic of whole societies. Sociologists since virtually the beginnings of their discipline have, in fact, repeatedly differentiated two broad types of societies within the seemingly endless diversity. Herbert Spencer labeled these types the *militant* and *industrial;* Sir Henry Maine distinguished between a society based on *status* and one based on *contract;* Ferdinand Tönnies differentiated *Gemeinschaft* (community) from *Gesellschaft* (society); Émile Durkheim contrasted societies held together by *mechanical solidarity* and those held together by *organic solidarity;* Howard Becker has identified the two types as *sacred* and *secular;* and Robert Redfield employs the categories of *folk* and *urban* society.

Each of these pairs of categories calls attention in different ways and with varying emphasis to approximately the same social and cultural differences. We can bring together these various contrasts within the more recently coined concepts of *communal* and *associational* societies.

A communal society is typically small, with a simple division of labor and consequently only a limited differentiation of roles. The role of the adult male among the Nunivak Eskimos, to take an extreme case, is roughly the same for almost all men, with some differences only among those who are married, single, or widowed; the only important economic differentiation is between men and women; the shaman alone performs a distinct religious role; and except for chiefs with limited authority and older men who exercise an unofficial and informal leadership, there is no formal structure of political roles. Families and other (informal) primary groups make up the important units within the society as a whole. Social roles are therefore in-clusive rather than segmental; they include many aspects of behavior rather than merely some limited segment of an individual's activities.

Because members of a communal society generally per-form inclusive rather than segmental roles, they necessarily interact with one another in a wide variety of contexts. Social relationships are therefore long-lasting, inclusive, and intimate or personal. They take on intrinsic significance rather than being instrumental; they are valued (positively or negatively) for themselves rather than as means to other ends. The reciprocal expectations of persons involved in these primary relationships are diffuse and generalized; one must live up to standards of respect, loyalty, affection, or love, for example, rather than merely fulfill specifically de-fined obligations.

Immediate families and often larger kin groups, small cliques, and perhaps a handful of other subdivisions ex-haust the group memberships in the communal type of society. There may be various kinds of organizations based on age, sex, or marital status, though even these are likely to be small primary groups rather than special interest asso-ciations. Thus among the Samoans were the *Fono,* the as-sembly of headmen of the village households; the *Aumaga,* the organization made up of younger men and those not yet recognized as headmen; and the *Auluma,* a loose organ-ization of unmarried women, widows, and wives of men not yet in the *Fono.*

In such a social structure behavior is regulated largely by custom; the many facets of everyday life are governed by a complex array of rules and regulations covering the activ-ities of eating and sleeping, hunting and fishing, praying and dancing, and love-making. Action flows fairly smoothly through conventional grooves. With mores exercising a strong hold upon behavior, there is little need for formal law. Law, we might say, is part of the tradition; it is not codified or rationalized, not enacted or dictated but, emerging from the cumulative experience of the society, is incorporated in the customs known and accepted by its members. The strong grip of tradition does not mean, however, an identity of behavior among men. As Redfield has pointed out, the individual is not a "sort of automaton in which custom is the mainspring. . . . Within the limits set by custom there is invitation to excel in performance. There is lively competition, a sense of opportunity, and a feeling that what the culture moves one to do is well worth doing." [25]

To summarize, in the communal society social roles are inclusive rather than segmental, social relationships are personal and intimate, and there are comparatively few subgroups other than family and kinship units. In this typically "small, isolated, nonliterate, and homogeneous [society], with a strong sense of group solidarity," [26] tradition permeates all aspects of life and the range of alternative patterns of behavior open to individuals is inevitably restricted.

The *associational society,* which is epitomized by the great modern metropolis, is characterized by a marked division of labor and a proliferation of social roles. Individuals must fit into a complex social structure in which they occupy many statuses and play many different and frequently unrelated roles. Whether one is a Catholic, a Protestant, or a Jew is (in principle, though not always in fact) irrelevant to the particular occupation one follows; treatment in a court of law is supposedly unaffected by one's political affiliations and activities, the clubs to which one belongs, and one's economic position. A man's wage or salary is not influenced by whether he is single or married, childless or father of a large brood. The various roles men play are usually segmental; they are limited to specific contexts, confined to a narrow range of activities, and involve the personality of the actor to a limited extent only.

Social relationships in the associational society therefore tend to be transitory, superficial, and impersonal. Individuals associate with one another for limited purposes and social interaction tends to be confined to the specific interests involved.

> The prototype is the narrowly contractual relation of buyer and seller in an open market exchange transaction, in which everything is formally irrelevant to the relation except considerations of price, quantity, and quality of the goods being exchanged. The rights and obligations of the parties are specific and definite—neither more nor less than explicitly agreed upon for the specific occasion—and the establishment of any particular associational relation does not imply any other social relations between the participants.[27]

Such relations are essentially instrumental; they are important not in themselves but for the goals or ends which they bring closer to realization. As a result there is less possibility of strong emotional involvement with other persons than in primary relationships.

Life in the associational society loses its unitary, cohesive character. The job and family life are seemingly separated, religion is apt to be confined to particular times and places instead of permeating the whole of human existence, work and leisure are sharply distinguished. As a result, the family does not occupy the same central place in the social structure that it possesses in a communal society. Men belong to various groups, and many of these are bureaucratically organized associations, each devoted to and pursuing its own goals and interests.

In this complex, diversified society, with its myriad groups and competing interests, the pervasive hold of tradition has been largely broken, and the comparative uniformity of thought has been replaced by an almost endless variety. There are relatively few universally accepted beliefs, values, and standards of behavior; the mores have been weakened, and formal law has emerged to regulate behavior and govern social intercourse. Change is therefore rapid; indeed, sophistication and innovation are positively sanctioned in many areas of life. Instead of the tight integration characteristic of communal society, the associational society is loosely articulated and the degree of consensus tends to diminish.

These ideal types suggest some of the ways in which the various elements of social organization are related to one another: As roles change from inclusive to segmental, social relationships tend to become more formal and impersonal; as interests multiply with the division of labor, associations proliferate; as the size of a society—or an association—increases, the tendency toward formal organization is encouraged. Such generalizations provide a useful starting point in the analysis of specific societies.

The distinction between communal and associational society also provides the basis for a historical interpretation of modern society. The long-run trend, some students argue, has been from communal to associational society. The growth of cities, the presumed decline in the importance of the family, the multiplication of associations and the extension of bureaucracy, the weakening of tradition, and the lessened role of religion in everyday life are all adduced as evidence of this transformation. These changes lead on the one hand to disorganization, conflict, instability, anxiety, and psychological strains, on the other hand to freedom from controls and coercion and to new opportunities for individual growth and creativity. This historical interpretation, therefore, is closely linked to both theoretical assertions and moral judgments about the importance of intimate relations, tradition, and common values, and their place in modern society.

The problems that are thus raised not only concern sociology, but also deal with crucial issues in the future of modern society. On what basis can consensus and stability be achieved in an urban industrial society? Is it necessary, in order to solve the social and economic problems of such a society, to return to traditional values and older modes of organization? Are the alternative social and cultural forms appropriate to a complex modern society consistent with such values as freedom, opportunity, and individuality?

Notes

[1] Charles H. Cooley, *Human Nature and the Social Order* (New York: Scribner, 1902), p. 33 *n.*

[2] Adam Ferguson, *Essay on the History of Civil Society* (7th ed.; Boston: Hastings, 1809), p. 4.

[3] For a review of the literature on feral man see M. F. Ashley Montagu, *The Direction of Human Development* (New York: Harper, 1955), Ch. 11. For a detailed description and analysis of a case of a completely rejected child see Kingsley Davis, "Extreme Social Isolation of a Child," *American Journal of Sociology,* XLV (January, 1940), 554–65; and "Final Note on a Case of Extreme Isolation," *American Journal of Sociology,* LII (March, 1947), 432–47. A more recent report on a case of feral man is found in William F. Ogburn, "The Wolf Boy of Agra," *American Journal of Sociology,* LXIV (March, 1959), 449–54. A suggestive psychological interpretation of feral man is offered by Bruno Bettelheim, "Feral Children and Autistic Children," *American Journal of Sociology,* LXIV (March, 1959), 455–67.

[4] For a detailed review of the meanings assigned to "culture," both past and present, see Alfred L. Kroeber and Clyde Kluckhohn, *Culture, a Critical Review of Concepts and Definitions* (New York: Random House Vintage Books, n.d.). For an account of the various ways in which "culture" has been used since the end of the eighteenth century and of its applications in social criticism rather than social science, see the stimulating and sugges-

tive study by Raymond Williams, *Culture and Society* (New York: Doubleday Anchor Books, 1959).

5 Gladys Bryson, *Man and Society* (Princeton: Princeton University Press, 1945).

6 Jay Rumney and Joseph Maier, *Sociology: The Science of Society* (New York: Schuman, 1953), p. 74.

7 Georg Simmel, *Sociology*, trans. by Kurt H. Wolff (New York: Free Press, 1950), p. 10.

8 Ralph Linton, *The Study of Man* (New York: Appleton, 1936), p. 91.

9 Ralph Linton, *The Cultural Background of Personality* (New York: Appleton, 1945), p. 125.

10 R. R. Marett, *Anthropology* (rev. ed.; London: Oxford, 1944), p. 183.

11 Talcott Parsons, *Essays in Sociological Theory* (New York: Free Press, 1949), p. 203.

12 William Graham Sumner, *Folkways* (Boston: Ginn, 1906), pp. 53-4.

13 See Kingsley Davis, *Human Society* (New York: Macmillan, 1949), p. 71.

14 Robert M. MacIver and Charles H. Page, *Society: An Introductory Analysis* (New York: Rinehart, 1949), p. 24.

15 John Kenneth Galbraith, *The Affluent Society* (Boston: Houghton Mifflin, 1958), p. 9.

16 Ernst Cassirer, *An Essay on Man* (New York: Doubleday Anchor Books, 1953), pp. 53-5.

17 A. L. Kroeber and Talcott Parsons, "The Concepts of Culture and of Social System," *American Sociological Review*, XXIII (October, 1958), 582-3.

18 See, for example, the selections by William Archer, Constant Coquelin, and Konstantin Stanislavsky in Toby Cole and Helen Krich Chinoy (eds.), *Actors on Acting* (New York: Crown, 1949).

19 Mirra Komarovsky, "Cultural Contradictions and Sex Roles," *American Journal of Sociology*, LII (November, 1946), 184-9.

[20] Ely Chinoy, "Local Union Leadership," in Alvin W. Gouldner (ed.), *Studies in Leadership* (New York: Harper, 1950), p. 168.

[21] Talcott Parsons, *The Social System* (New York: Free Press, 1951), pp. 439–47.

[22] For an amusing characterization of the *tummler* see David Boroff, "The Catskills: Still Having Wonderful Time," *Harper's Magazine*, July, 1958, pp. 56–63.

[23] Morris Ginsberg, *Sociology* (London: Butterworth, 1934), pp. 40–1.

[24] For a description of such an urban neighborhood, see Michael Young and Peter Willmott, *Family and Kinship in East London* (New York: Free Press, 1957).

[25] Robert Redfield, "The Folk Society," *American Journal of Sociology*, LII (January, 1947), 300.

[26] *Ibid.*, p. 297.

[27] Robin M. Williams, Jr., *American Society* (2nd ed.; New York: Knopf, 1960), pp. 479–80.

Suggestions for further reading

GOFFMAN, ERVING. *The Presentation of Self in Everyday Life*. Garden City: Doubleday Anchor Books, 1959.
A sensitive and perceptive analysis of role-playing and social interaction seen from the perspective of a "dramatic performance."

GREER, SCOTT. *Social Organization*. New York: Random House, 1955.
A suggestive discussion that sees social organization as both structure and process.

HUGHES, EVERETT C. "Dilemmas and Contradictions of Status," *American Journal of Sociology*, L (March, 1945), 353–9.
A good brief description of problems stemming from situations in which men are placed in incompatible roles.

KLUCKHOHN, CLYDE, AND WILLIAM H. KELLEY. "The Concept of Culture," in Ralph Linton (ed.), *The Science of Man in the*

World Crisis. New York: Columbia University Press, 1945, pp. 78–106.
A conversation in which several anthropologists explore the concept of culture.

KOMAROVSKY, MIRRA. "Cultural Contradictions and Sex Roles," *American Journal of Sociology,* LII (November, 1946), 184–9.
An analysis of the difficulties faced by college women because of the competing demands of different roles they play.

MAC IVER, ROBERT M. The Web of Government. New York: Macmillan, 1947, pp. 421–30.
A penetrating summary of the chief characteristics of the "multigroup" (associational) society.

REDFIELD, ROBERT. *The Little Community.* Chicago: University of Chicago Press, 1960.
A seminal analysis of the folk (communal) society by a noted anthropologist.

SUMNER, WILLIAM GRAHAM. *Folkways.* Boston: Ginn, 1906.
The pioneer description of folkways and mores. The gist of the analysis is found in Chapter I; the remainder of the book is largely illustrative and based on materials now substantially out of date.

WILLIAMS, ROBIN M., JR. *American Society.* 2nd ed. New York: Knopf, 1960, Ch. 12.
A statement of the chief characteristics of social organization and an attempt to describe the outlines of social organization in the United States.

ZNANIECKI, FLORIAN. *Social Relations and Social Roles.* San Francisco: Chandler, 1965.
A segment of an unfinished treatise by one of the major figures in the development of sociology that explores in detail the nature and variety of social relationships and social roles.

3

diversity and uniformity

The variety of social forms

Both culture and social organization display an almost endless variety of forms, a fact that raises many questions and
suggests numerous hypotheses of great importance in sociological inquiry. In an age when the rest of the world is daily
brought close by modern means of transportation and communication, the enormous diversity of customs, beliefs,
habits, and forms of social organization found in human
society hardly seems to need elaborate documentation. The
veiling of Moslem women, the strange customs of the Eskimos, love in the south seas, Communist political and economic arrangements—these and many other examples of

traditions, practices, and social structures that differ from our own are continually reported in the press, radio, and television and, for those who are interested, described in books that are easily available. Yet the prevailing tendency to measure all other customs against our own is so strong that the extent and manner of diversity require constant emphasis.

The full range of cultural and social variation can be found in the vast library of anthropological studies, the reports of perceptive travelers and journalists, and the accounts of the past offered by historians. One is tempted to choose examples of either the trivial or the exotic, the very commonplace and familiar or the most unusual and bizarre, in order to demonstrate how widely human behavior can vary and, incidentally, to stimulate the reader to develop and sustain objectivity in examining his own culture and society. For unusual examples of what others take to be normal or conventional may lead us to look with fresh eyes upon those customs generally taken for granted.

The Andaman Islanders in the Bay of Bengal are not supposed to whistle at night because they believe it will attract spirits; among Americans whistling is supposed to be one way of keeping up one's spirits while walking alone past a graveyard at night. Among the Comanche, brothers may, under certain circumstances, lend their wives to each other for sexual purposes, and certain Eskimo groups characteristically offer their wives for the night to a visitor, practices that Americans and many others would look upon as highly immoral. Hindus refuse to eat beef and Moslems to eat pork, whereas Christians, except for a small group of vegetarians, enjoy both. Among the Toda of South India, to thumb one's nose at another person is a sign of respect; in Western Europe and the United States, to do so is a gesture that expresses defiance and disrespect. Americans and Europeans shake hands by way of greeting; Polynesians rub noses.

These striking illustrations should not lead us to ignore more familiar but less obvious social and cultural differences, which at close range seem to be matters merely of individual preference and personality characteristics. Interest in symphonic music is widespread among some groups in the United States, but Kentucky mountaineers, urban Negro workers, and teen-agers are likely to prefer other kinds of music. Rural folk tend to identify the evening meal as "supper" and urbanites as "dinner," although some city dwellers, particularly in the working class, may retain the rural usage. Class consciousness seems to be more pervasive among the very rich than among other economic groups. Americans with high incomes tend to be Republicans whereas those with low incomes are more frequently Democrats.

The existence of marked differences in the norms, values, and social arrangements found in societies scattered around the world—and within societies—not only raises the scientific question of how to account for social and cultural diversity; it also poses ethical or moral problems that require at least brief comment here. People everywhere tend to consider their own values and beliefs absolute. But if there are marked differences in the rules and values governing family life, sexual behavior, political relationships and practices, economic activities, religious ritual and dogma, and so on, can there be any absolute standards? "The mores," wrote William Graham Sumner, "can make anything right and anything wrong." On what grounds— if any—is it possible to conclude that one set of norms and beliefs is right and another wrong? One possible answer would be the existence of universally held standards. Perhaps the closest approximation to a universal norm is the incest taboo; yet even though sexual relations between siblings and between parents and children are always forbidden (except in a few special situations), there is considerable variation in the other relatives who are included within the taboo.

From the facts of cultural variation has emerged the principle of cultural relativity, that beliefs and norms valid in one society may be looked upon as false or immoral in another. The principle clearly conflicts with any assertion of absolute truth and has sometimes been attacked as subversive of established belief and even of the maintenance of social order. As is so often the case, however, the same ideas can be used in very different ways. From one point of view, it is true, cultural relativity can provide the basis for a radical critique of existing practices and beliefs. If other peoples seem to live adequately and happily under different norms and with different beliefs, then perhaps one's own culture is not the best or free from defects. If the Samoans allow or encourage premarital sexual intercourse without disastrous results or even with desirable consequences, then perhaps the conventional sexual mores of American society could be changed for the better. If economic activities can be pursued without the stress of competition, then perhaps the widespread assumption that competition is inevitable and is the source of progress is not true.

This kind of radical critique, which was once widespread, has been tempered by recognition of the fact that single beliefs or practices cannot be properly interpreted or evaluated without reference to the total context in which they are embedded. If Samoan sexual practices did not produce destructive consequences, it was because of other aspects of Samoan culture and social structure. Borrowing of individual cultural traits is difficult because of the close interdependence of the elements of a culture. From these considerations it would appear that cultural relativity can also lead to a conservative attitude toward norms and values. If culture is relative, then whatever exists in one's own society is clearly appropriate—for that society—and need not be questioned. If the Samoans believe in and practice premarital sexual exploration, then it may be good for them, but it has no implications for appropriate practice elsewhere. The desirability of American Puritanical sexual mores then can only be assessed within the confines of American culture and society; the experience of other societies would appear to be irrelevant. This inference from the doctrine of cultural relativity is as limited as the radical critique which rejected some norms or values out of hand without reference to the total context in which they were located.

The resolution of the conflict between any type of cultural absolutism and cultural relativity and an evaluation of all the moral or ethical implications of cultural relativity clearly pose such complex issues that we can hardly explore them here in any detail. But cultural relativity does lead to at least one important conclusion upon which there may be considerable agreement: that each society, with its norms and values, is one of many, capable of change—in various directions—and is a product of man's effort to come to terms with the world around him and with the needs of an ongoing social order. The awareness of cultural diversity is thus an antidote to ethnocentrism and the basis for a fuller understanding of mankind's common humanity.

Social uniformities

Within the diversity and variety, however, are many kinds of uniformities. On the basis of data in the Human Relations Area Files at Yale University, George Murdock has compiled a list of those features

> which occur, so far as the author's knowledge goes, in every culture known to history or ethnography: age-grading, athletic sports, bodily adornment, calendar, cleanliness training, com-

munity organization, cooking, cooperative labor, cosmology, courtship, dancing, decorative art, divination, division of labor, dream interpretation, education, eschatology, ethics, ethnobotany, etiquette, faith healing, family, feasting, fire-making, folklore, food taboos, funeral rites, games, gestures, gift giving, government, greetings, hair styles, hospitality, housing, hygiene, incest taboos, inheritance rules, joking, kin-groups, kinship nomenclature, language, law, luck super-stitions, magic, marriage, mealtimes, medicine, modesty con-cerning natural functions, mourning, music, mythology, numerals, obstetrics, penal sanctions, personal names, popula-tion policy, postnatal care, pregnancy usages, property rights, propitiation of supernatural beings, puberty customs, reli-gious ritual, residence rules, sexual restrictions, soul concepts, status differentiation, surgery, tool making, trade, visiting, weaning, and weather control.[1]

This list, of course, represents a set of abstractions within the broad category of culture, although it includes, clearly, forms of social organization as well (family, kin-groups, status differentiation, division of labor). The list could be both expanded and contracted, and other types of uni-formities could be substituted; there is no final classification of the elements of culture and social organization. Clark Wissler, for example, describes the universal components of culture as consisting of speech, material traits, art, mythology and scientific thinking, religion, family and so-cial systems, property, government, and war.[2] In their classic descriptions of "Middletown," a midwestern Amer-ican community, Robert and Helen Lynd utilized a set of categories derived from Wissler: getting a living, making a home, training the young, using leisure, engaging in re-ligious practices, and participating in community activities (including government).[3] Couched in other terms, one finds in all societies a family system, a structure of power and authority, religious beliefs and practices, and institutions which govern the allocation and use of scarce resources (economic institutions). The universal elements in culture and society can therefore be identified at different levels of abstraction; the varieties of social life can be categorized or conceptualized in different terms. The explanations which are consequently offered for the regularities and patterns found in social life may then depend on which categories are used.

In addition to universal social and cultural patterns there are also those forms which recur only in some cases. Bureaucracy as a type of social organization is found in all modern industrial societies and, to a limited extent, in some "primitive" societies. Historically it has also appeared in ancient Egypt, classical China, the Roman Empire, and the medieval (and modern) Catholic Church. Similarly, the institutions labeled as "feudal" have existed in many times and areas: medieval Europe, modern Islam, premodern Japan, parts of Latin America. Monogamy is a widespread pattern, but many societies encourage other forms of marriage. Age-grading occurs in a number of societies, as do the levirate (the requirement that a man marry his dead brother's widow), cross-cousin marriage, and inheritance only through the mother's (or only the father's) family. Though some are frequent, none of these patterns is universal.

A major task of sociology is to account for both the diversity to be found in social life and for the recurrent elements in culture and social organization. Why is an incest taboo universally found? Or religion? Or magic? Or status differentiation? Or the division of labor? Why do groups differ from one another in the objects which they worship? In their sexual practices? In the distribution of power and authority? In the organization of economic activities? But societies that differ in many respects also exhibit similar cultural patterns and forms of social organization. The United States and the Soviet Union are dissimilar in many ways, yet both possess highly developed technologies, elaborate bureaucratic organization, and a steadily increasing concentration of the population in urban areas. Virtually all the countries of western Europe and the United States experienced a rise in the birth rate after the end of World War II, yet their family systems differ in many respects. The similarities, as well as the differences, call for explanation.

Human history is full of alternative theories that try to interpret these facts. A sociological explanation, we contend, is the most fruitful way of accounting for both the recurrent features of social life and for the differences among and within societies. But so widespread and pervasive are nonsociological theories, particularly those which emphasize biological and geographical facts, that they should be reviewed and evaluated.

Biology and society

The universal recurrence of certain types of cultural patterns and forms of social organization suggests the possibility of a close relationship between them and the biological nature of man. Even if culture is learned, rather than inherited, is it possible that what is learned depends upon innate characteristics? Phrased somewhat differently, to what extent or in what ways are culture and social organization determined, shaped, or influenced by man's biologically inherited equipment, impulses, and drives? Is there an "instinct" for family life? Or for religious belief and practice? Does the incest taboo occur universally because of some innate revulsion against sexual contact with members of one's own family? Are people inherently modest about their biological functions? Do men naturally seek to acquire possessions or to gain power over others?

Given their diversity, culture and social organization can hardly be shaped or molded by inherited tendencies, except perhaps in the most general fashion. Although all societies have some kind of family system, the variations in size, marital arrangements, and division of responsibilities among members, and in the norms governing descent, inheritance, residence, and relations among kin rule out the likelihood that innate characteristics *determine* the nature of family organization. The fact that there are only two sexes and not three or four obviously sets limits on the forms of marriage: monogamy, polygyny (one man and more than one woman), polyandry (one woman and more than one man), and group marriage (a menage of several men and several women, a pattern found so infrequently that some scholars deny its existence). But which of these forms a group adopts depends upon culture, not inherited impulses. The family is rooted in biological fact, to be sure, but its forms cannot be explained biologically.

The enormous range of sacred beliefs, objects, and practices similarly demonstrates the lack of specific inherited patterns of religious behavior. All kinds of objects are worshiped or given religious significance: animals, trees, plants, the sun and moon, particular persons, ancestors, spirits, and many kinds of gods. Religious observances encompass all manner of action and ritual. But, it may be argued, even if no specific religious forms are inherent or instinctive, the prevalence of religion in all societies would surely seem to demonstrate some innate need or impulse in man's nature.

The Soviet Union, it has been claimed, provides a test case which demonstrates the inherent need for some religion, for the Soviet government has tried to extinguish religion, only to fail. Not only is there evidence of continued religious faith and practice, but Communism itself, it is said, has become a new "secular" religion. It seems clear, however, that traditional religion maintains its hold chiefly among older Soviet citizens, and it is still possible that continued antireligious agitation eventually may virtually eliminate traditional religion in the Soviet Union; deep-rooted beliefs are hardly to be destroyed in a short time. The presumed religious character of Communism itself remains to be fully demonstrated. Communism cannot be considered a religion if it merely serves the same functions; for if religion is defined simply by the functions it serves, it becomes impossible to distinguish religious from other beliefs and practices that explain or interpret the character of human life and its relations to the divine, or that bind men together in a morally united community.

In any case, there are in many, perhaps in all, societies nonbelievers who reject or deny the prevailing religious views; despite the popular aphorism, there are atheists in fox-holes. (In a survey of American soldiers during the Second World War, 17 per cent of a group serving in the Pacific and 8 per cent of a group in Italy reported that prayer did not "help at all when the going was rough." [4]) It seems more consistent with the facts available to us, therefore, to conclude that there is no biologically determined inevitability about the emergence of religious belief and practice. In the long run there is, perhaps, a strong tendency for religion to emerge from man's search for answers to certain fundamental problems of human existence, answers usually shared within a group, but at any time and place the extent, degree, and form of religious belief may vary enormously.

From these illustrations and from the knowledge provided by psychology and biology, it seems clear that the impulses or drives, the potentialities for emotional response and learning, are so general and diffuse that they can be molded or channeled in the innumerable ways which an inspection of human societies reveals. As we have pointed out earlier, the *absence* of specific inherited modes of behavior makes possible the development of culture and the substantial variation in the means by which men insure their survival and regulate their relations with one another.

The social insects—ants, bees, and others—cannot vary their behavior because their responses and the roles they play are rooted in instinct; in the complex social life of the beehive, each participant obeys the dictates of his genetic character. Nonhuman primates—chimpanzees, howler monkeys, baboons, and others—are less constrained by instinct than insects and possess a considerable capacity for learning. But they are limited in their behavior and social development by the absence of culture, a lack which stems largely from their inability to learn or acquire an abstract language. Most primates possess or learn a substantial vocabulary of signs by which they can communicate, although both the range of sounds they can utter and their capacity for abstraction are greatly limited. The biological characteristics which distinguish man from other animals—the upright stance, opposable thumb, larger and more highly developed brain, and the capacity for language—are conditions necessary for culture; they do not account for it.

Other biological facts, however, provide "points of reference" or "foci" around which cultural patterns and social structures inevitably develop. These foci consist of the structural and functional differences between the sexes; the fact that human infants are dependent for a comparatively long time upon others for survival; the organic drives generated by hunger, thirst, and sex; the processes of maturation and aging; and the fact of death. Around these points of reference develop standards governing the relations between the sexes, practices of child care, techniques for securing and preparing food and drink, funeral practices, puberty rites, and so on. In every society men and women, children and adults, have different roles to play. But the norms men obey and the roles they perform—the foods they eat, whether women are modest or flaunt their charms, techniques of child care, how readily children obey their parents, and whether the dead are cremated or buried, worshiped or merely mourned—depend not upon instinct but upon the nature of the society in which men live and its institutional prescriptions. "Human biology," Clyde Kluckhohn has said, "sets limits, supplies potentialities and drives, provides clues which cultures neglect or elaborate." [5]

Race

If biological facts cannot in themselves adequately explain the universally found types of institutions and social structures in human society, perhaps they may account for the differences which exist. It can be argued that the social and cultural differences among the peoples of the world stem from inherent biological differences, that the distinctive qualities of particular groups are hereditary. The lower level of education and economic achievement among American Negroes, some advocates of white supremacy have claimed, stems from an inevitable, biologically based inferiority. Americans and Englishmen possess and value democratic political institutions, it has been asserted, because of an innate predisposition and talent for self-government.[6] Chinese, Russians, French, Germans, and other nations presumably inherit particular talents and characteristics. "Through *my* race," wrote an eminent Mexican painter about one of his works, "will speak the Spirit."

The idea that cultural and social differences stem from or are determined by biological differences, an idea that came to a tragic harvest in recent years, has a long history, although its fullest, most systematic and influential elaboration is hardly more than a century old. Aristotle saw the differences between rulers and ruled, between Greeks, Asiatics, and northern Europeans, as inherent and natural. "For some men are by nature formed to be under the government of a master; others, of a king; others, to be the citizens of a free state, just and useful." [7] The explicit formulation of a theory which divides mankind into distinctive races, how-

ever, came only in the eighteenth century, when the great
Swedish botanist Linnaeus identified four races on the
basis of skin color: *Americanus rufus, Europaeus albus,
Asiaticus luridus,* and *Afer niger.* In addition he established
a category which he labeled "monstrosus," to include
abnormal types with which he was not familiar.[8] These
categories, of course, have since been refined and elaborated
by biologists and physical anthropologists. The attempt to
link these biological differences to social and cultural variations occurred in the nineteenth century, largely in the
work of Count Arthur de Gobineau, a French aristocrat
who, with his follower, Houston Stewart Chamberlain,
inadvertently provided the theoretical foundations for Nazi-
racist doctrine and practice.

As a biological concept, race refers to a number of
people who possess common inherited characteristics. Most
racial classifications are based on external physical traits:
color of the skin, hair, and eyes, head form, type of hair,
contours of the nose and jaw, height, body build, amount
of body hair. The racial interpretation of social and cultural
variation asserts that these biological characteristics account for the level and nature of a particular culture, the
form of government, or the frequency of various patterns
of behavior. According to such theories, European civilization was superior to that of the rest of the world because
of the innate superiority of the white man. Negroes have
a higher rate of venereal disease and illegitimacy in the
United States than whites, such a theory holds, because of
their innate immorality. Whatever distinct qualities are
attributed to the Jews (who have been identified both as
evil capitalists and evil Communists, as a menace to others
because they are superior or because they are inferior) are
traced to hereditary capabilities. Such theories gain a seem-
ing plausibility because there are some empirical correlations between racial characteristics and cultural and social
forms. It is possible to point to actual differences in be-

havior, beliefs, values, and social organization between groups that are radically more or less distinct, between tall, blond, blue-eyed Nordics and short, dark, brown-eyed Mediterraneans, between white Europeans and black Africans, between yellow-skinned Chinese and white-skinned Americans. It is then an easy, though not legitimate, step from these obvious facts to the conclusion that racial traits *determine* cultural and social characteristics.

The evidence against this racial determinism is extremely strong. There are, first, serious technical problems in establishing racial classifications and in placing individuals in these categories. The biological traits used in identifying races vary widely, within groups as well as between them. Some nominally "white" Europeans are darker than some presumably "black" Africans. Many "tall" Nordics are actually shorter than the generally shorter Mediterranean. "With each character chosen for measurement, though the averages differ, the extremes overlap." [9] In addition, the physical features used for racial classification do not occur in stable relationships. Black-skinned peoples are among the shortest and tallest; white-skinned people have both very long heads (dolichocephalic) and very round heads (brachycephalic). In a study done in Sweden in 1897–1898 it was found that only 11 per cent conformed to the "pure" tall, blue-eyed, blond, long-headed Nordic type, although the Swedes are considered to be one of the most Nordic of European populations.[10]

Human history is full of racial mixing and the present racial categories typically include many individuals who are not racially "pure." The great migrations in human history frequently brought one physical type into close contact with another, with inevitable intermixture. No European nation is racially distinct; "white" Americans are a complex mixture of darker and lighter groups, all of whom nominally belong to the same race. Many, probably most, Americans who are labeled as Negro (and many "whites" as well) actually possess a mixed racial ancestry, for there has been considerable miscegenation in the past. "Because of the complexity of human history," a recent statement on race by a group of distinguished physical anthropologists and biologists concluded, "there are . . . many populations which cannot easily be fitted into a racial classification." [11]

Despite the existence of racially mixed populations, or *clines,* as they are technically identified, a large proportion of the world's population probably falls into recognizable racial categories. A recent major study, which sought to describe the world's races, assigned over 90 per cent to the Caucasoid and Mongoloid races and the remaining to the Negroid, Australoid, and Capoid. Clinal populations were distributed on the basis of their "parent races." Both the numerical and geographical distribution and many of the attributes of these races were looked upon as historical as well as biological products, with "distinctive genetic attributes" emerging "through the selective forces of all aspects of the environment, including culture." [12]

Even though it may thus be possible to establish clearly differentiated races and to place each person unambiguously in one or the other of these races, there is still no evidence of any connection between racial traits and the forms of social life. Anthropological, sociological, and historical data provide overwhelming testimony that similar cultures can be found among peoples with very different physical characteristics, and that culture and social organization can change quickly without any corresponding change in racial identity. Nordics have lived under totalitarian political institutions and under democratic ones. During the period around World War I many American writers maintained that the Teutonic peoples have peculiar instinctive talents for self-government; during the 1930s, Hitler created a totalitarian state and justified his actions on the grounds of the innate superiority of the Nordic race. In Africa, hitherto primitive peoples have been transformed under our very eyes into modern national states that are increasingly playing an important role on the world scene.

To put the matter in homelier and perhaps more concrete terms, French cuisine is different from American or English not because of innate culinary talents but because of different cultural and social backgrounds. Hindus refuse to eat beef not because they are naturally superstitious and ignorant, but because they hold cows to be sacred. The permissive or approving attitudes toward premarital sexual experience found in many societies are not the product of innate immorality or of a lower stage of human development but of social and cultural circumstances. If most Negroes in the United States have comparatively little education and hold inferior jobs, it is not because they possess little aptitude for education or are less capable of skilled work and of assuming responsibility, but because of the disabilities to which their social position in American society exposes them.

Although skin color, shape of the head, size, and other presumably racial traits do not *determine* what people eat or think or how they are ruled, these physical characteristics cannot be totally excluded from sociological analysis. They can provide some of the biological "clues" that a culture seizes upon and uses. Men may develop attitudes and feelings toward skin color; they may respond favorably or unfavorably to the shape of the eyelid. They may order their relationships on the basis of racial differences, confining those with dark skins to menial jobs, or excluding them from schools, or from certain forms of social intercourse. They may justify such behavior with complex theories of race, or with Biblical citations to prove that God intended white and black to be separate. Physical appearance, then, becomes an element the sociological significance of which depends upon the sentiments and values assigned to it. (Not only racial characteristics but other physical traits as well, it should be noted, often come to have social meaning. The present standards of feminine attractiveness in America, for example, emphasize relatively svelte, sleek lines: among the Ibo of West Africa, feminine beauty "is all but identified with obesity." A society may seek to cultivate the physical aptitudes of the warrior or athlete, or it may minimize these attributes in favor of artistic or intellectual abilities, or it may stress both to varying degrees.)

Popular conceptions of race must therefore be distinguished from the tested knowledge arrived at through scientific investigation. The sociological analysis of racial ideas is different from the biological analysis of racial characteristics. Sociologists are concerned with the opinions and attitudes of people with regard to race and toward specific racial groups and how they affect behavior and social structure. Biologists and physical anthropologists seek to discover the genetic character of human races, insofar as they exist, and to find out whether each race possesses any distinctive traits or abilities. There are, it appears, racially linked traits; for example, only Negroes can suffer from a disease called sickle cell anemia, but as we have seen, there is little evidence that skin color, hair form, or any of the many other biological attributes that have been thus examined exert any determining influence on culture or social organization.

The ideas to which men have subscribed, however, have played a very important historical role. Although they do not constitute the total explanation for the extermination of six million Jews by the Nazis, who considered Jews an inferior race, or of racial segregation in the United States, England, the Union of South Africa, and elsewhere, racial —or perhaps more accurately, racist—ideologies can justify or rationalize the treatment of particular racial and ethnic groups. In time, scientifically established facts and theories may gain popular currency, as they seem to be doing in some areas and among some groups, replacing myth, tradition, and folklore. Such a transition will, of course, have its own sociological consequences.

Sex differences

We have thus far reduced biological facts to a secondary role in the explanation of sociological phenomena—to the status of relevant conditions rather than determining factors. Can we also minimize in this fashion the differences between men and women? To what extent is their behavior determined by inherited characteristics linked with their sex? The considerable variation in the roles played by men and women in different societies suggests the possibility that, except for childbearing, there are no inherent differences, that maleness and femaleness, male roles and female roles, depend solely upon what the culture makes of them. The differences that do exist in attitudes, interests, and behavior seem in many instances readily explicable by reference to cultural facts—the ways in which children are reared and the expectations attached to men and women. American girls are given dolls, encouraged to be "little mothers" and to behave like "little ladies." They are rewarded when they behave in a "feminine" fashion and are likely to be scolded if they try to ape their male playmates or siblings. Boys, on the other hand, are given toy guns or mechanical gadgets and are expected to be aggressive; they are more likely to be allowed to get dirty without being scolded, to run, jump, climb, and in various other ways to behave like a "real boy." Failure to live up to these expectations leads to the unpleasant epithet of "sissy" and to other pressures to conform to the appropriate masculine behavior. Little wonder that women usually behave like ladies and men usually behave like men.

Yet despite the evidence that sex differences are apparently in many ways cultural rather than biological products, there remain enough recurrent and widespread differences between men and women to refute an all-embracing cultural determinism. In every society different roles are assigned to men and women, and there is some sexual division of labor. The care of young children is almost everywhere the task of women, who rarely participate in military combat, metalworking, hunting, or fishing. Although the father often gives children a great deal of attention—playing with them, fondling them, looking after their needs—the nurturing role, described explicitly in our society as "mothering," is characteristically filled by the mother. There are cases of female soldiers—in Russia and Israel in recent times, in parts of Africa in the past, and the legendary Amazons—but they are very much the exception.

Levels and types of achievement are also significantly different among the sexes. History has seen comparatively few women of great distinction in art, letters, politics, science, and philosophy. There are—and have been—many women of talent who have made significant contributions to these fields, but the towering figures—Dante, Newton, Goethe, Kant, Picasso, Freud, Einstein—have been almost without exception men.

Differences in the expected behavior of men and women are often linked to obvious contrasts in personality. Although there are "masculine" women and "effeminate" men, as well as a few societies in which women take over what we would define as the masculine role and personality,[13] men are on the whole more aggressive and dominating, and many cultures expressly consign women to a subordinate and inferior status.

Finally, despite the greater strength and endurance of the male, women seem to be in some respects biologically superior. Not only do they mature earlier, physically, emotionally, and intellectually, but they are also less susceptible to disease, have lower mortality rates, and enjoy a longer life expectancy.

Are all these differences due solely to culture and society, or do they stem, at least in part, from the complex interaction between inherent characteristics and cultural patterns? There is no clear answer to these questions. We do not know the extent to which—and how—physiological and anatomical characteristics of each sex and their accompanying psychological traits, if any, shape sex roles. In a suggestive essay, Erich Fromm argues that there is a "coloring of character which is rooted in sex differences" derived from such things as the fact that sexual intercourse is always a test of a man's capacity, whereas a woman need not demonstrate anything but must only be willing to participate. Fromm adds, however, "This coloring is insignificant in comparison with the socially rooted differences, but it must not be entirely neglected." [14] There is indeed evidence that the psychological differences derived from biological characteristics can be so overlaid with cultural demands that their influence may not be readily apparent, at least to superficial observation, or is reflected only at deep psychological levels. Culture may virtually reverse the usual roles of men and women, though possibly at some psychological cost to both. The perhaps "natural" submissiveness of women, for example, may be replaced by culturally sanctioned aggressiveness, but if women are in fact passive and receptive, as some writers have claimed, then one might anticipate widely ramifying psychological and sociological consequences.

The debate over the "natural" differences between men and women and the "true" characteristics of each is not purely academic. Just as race may be a socially significant idea, so may varying definitions of "femininity" and "masculinity" affect sex roles and the relations between the sexes. Thus Betty Friedan argues, in her widely read and controversial *The Feminine Mystique,* that various sociological and psychological theories that define feminine fulfillment as essentially and naturally sexual and domestic are "self-fulfilling prophecies" that ignore the other activities and interests of which women are capable.[15]

It seems clear, then, that no sociological explanation can disregard such biological facts as race and sex or the conceptions that people have of these facts—but that sociology cannot be reduced to biology. Though the distinctive features of the human species make culture possible, they do not determine its content. Though nature imposes requirements of food, drink, shelter, and sexual gratification, it does not determine how they shall be met. Racial characteristics may influence men's behavior, but only because of the values men assign to them, and not because they are biologically tied to any precisely defined modes of action.

Climate and geography

A second major alternative to a sociological analysis of patterned behavior and group life emphasizes the role of the physical environment. Climatic and geographic interpretations of social life have a long history, dating back, as do most theories of man and society, at least to the ancient Greeks. For a full illustration of a theory which assigns primary importance to climatic variation we may turn to the eighteenth-century French philosopher Montesquieu:

> We have already observed that great heat enervates the strength and courage of men, and that in cold climates they have a certain vigour of body and mind, which renders them patient and intrepid, and qualifies them for arduous enterprises. This remark holds good, not only between different nations, but even in the different parts of the same country. In the north of China people are more courageous than those in the south; and those in the south of Corea have less bravery than those in the north.

We ought not, then, to be astonished that the effeminacy of the people in hot climates has almost always rendered them slaves; and that the bravery of those in cold climates has enabled them to maintain their liberties. This is an effect which springs from a natural cause. . . .

These facts being laid down, I reason thus: Asia has properly no temperate zone, as the places situated in a very cold climate immediately touch upon those which are exceedingly hot—that is, Turkey, Persia, India, China, Corea, and Japan.

In Europe, on the contrary, the temperate zone is very extensive, though situated in climates widely different from each other; there being no affinity between the climates of Spain and Italy and those of Norway and Sweden. But as the climate grows insensibly cold upon our advancing from south to north, nearly in proportion to the latitude of each country, it thence follows that each resembles the country adjoining it; that there is no very extraordinary difference between them, and that . . . the temperate zone is very extensive.

Hence it comes that in Asia the strong nations are opposed to the weak; the warlike, brave, and active peoples touch immediately upon those who are indolent, effeminate, and timorous; the one must, therefore, conquer, and the other be conquered. In Europe, on the contrary, strong nations are opposed to the strong, and those who join each other have nearly the same courage. This is the grand reason for the weakness of Asia, and of the strength of Europe; of the liberty of Europe, and of the slavery of Asia. . . .[16]

The facts upon which this interpretation rests can, of course, be challenged in the light of modern knowledge, but there remain a good many empirical correlations between climate and culture and social organization which lend credence to climatic determinism. Crime, suicide, and marriage rates vary during the year, being higher in some seasons and lower in others. Obviously life in the Arctic is different from that in Bali; life in the Sahara from that in tropical jungles.

The facts of topography, soil conditions, and natural resources supply yet another possible explanation of cultural and social differences. Thus a distinguished geographer has explained the form of most of the world's cities by reference to the topography and soil of the places where they have been built.[17] The presence of the English Channel has been cited frequently as the cause of many of England's distinctive features. The presence or absence of natural resources has been taken as the crucial factor in determining a nation's character and standing in the world of nations.

The evidence against both climatic and geographical determinism is clear and convincing. Widely dissimilar climates and geographical conditions have seen much the same pattern of culture and social organization. The perhaps apocryphal story of the Englishman dressing for dinner in the tropics illustrates this point, as does the historical evidence on the extent to which Europeans and, more recently, Americans have brought their ways of life to the various parts of the globe in which they have settled. June is the favored month for marriage in the United States, but some European peasant societies have preferred November. Conversely, climate and geography have remained the same in many areas in which marked changes have occurred in culture and social organization. The rapid transformation of societies as different as Russia and that of the Manus of the Admiralty Islands of the Pacific may serve as examples. Russia has changed in less than fifty years from a largely peasant society with only the beginnings of industrialization into a heavily urban, industrial society of the first rank. Within a period of barely ten years the Manus gave up a large part of their traditional culture and social structure as they adopted new customs, beliefs, and practices derived primarily from Americans brought to the Southwestern Pacific by World War II.[18]

Like biological facts, however, geographic and climatic

facts cannot be dismissed from the analysis of social and cultural life. People everywhere have some form of dress or bodily adornment, but the Eskimos wear furs to protect themselves from the cold while Tahitians wear only a loincloth or kilt of tapa cloth made from the bark of the mulberry tree. Climate and topography may not determine how people behave, but they set problems that must be solved. There is no necessary uniformity in how these problems are met; one can endure tropical climate by stripping to a loincloth, by sleeping through the hottest part of the day, or by developing and utilizing air-conditioning apparatus.

How people respond to heat or cold, mountainous terrain or level plains, how they utilize the resources they have or meet the problems created by the absence of resources, depends on their cultural equipment—their knowledge, skills, and values—and their social organization. A recent Air Force investigation of responses to climatic conditions reported that ". . . studies of Eskimos produced no evidence that their bodies were better equipped for the cold than those of the white men who are infiltrating their domain. The Eskimos' ability to endure extremely low temperatures seems to be based solely on acquired skills and excellently adapted clothing and diet." [19]

As we examine the world political scene, such geographic facts as the presence of oil deposits, the availability of tin, rubber, and uranium, and the amount of cultivable land possessed by each nation are of obvious significance. But it is important to note that they take on significance because of the values assigned to them. Their usefulness depends upon the knowledge and technology possessed by men. The Middle East was much less important in world affairs when navies did not burn oil; it may become less important as we develop atom-powered ships. The coal deposits of Pennsylvania and the iron ore of the Mesabi range in Minnesota had no significance or value for the aboriginal American Indians; modern Americans have erected an industrial civilization upon them.

Not only is geography unable to determine the form of society or shape its culture, it may itself be affected by human action, for men can change to some degree the physical environment in which they live. Agricultural practices can lead to the erosion of once fertile soil; witness the present state of the Tigris and Euphrates valleys, once the center of a flourishing agriculture and a great civilization. Unrestrained leveling of forests can lead to excessive run-off of water and damaging floods. But if men can create deserts they can also make the desert bloom, as the Israelis have done in once barren areas of their tiny nation. Rivers can be rechanneled, dams built, arid lands irrigated, mountains lowered, and tunnels built. As man leaves his imprint on soil, topography, and the flow of waters, the impact of these natural circumstances upon society is changed.

Conclusion

Biology, geography, and climate therefore have no independent significance in any explanation of the form and content of culture and social organization. They are clearly relevant, socially and culturally, at many points as necessary conditions and as circumstances which impose limits, set problems, provide opportunities. But the central focus of any analysis of the differences and uniformities found as one compares or examines cultural norms and social structures must remain on a distinctively sociological level. "We must . . . seek the explanation of social life in the nature of society itself," wrote the influential and distinguished French sociologist, Émile Durkheim.[20] Sociology, we have said, cannot be reduced to biology; nor can it be translated into either geography or meteorology. It contains a variety of theories within itself, but these all share the premise that sociology possesses a distinctive subject matter and point of view which are independent of the theories and perspectives of other disciplines.

There remains, however, one final problem to which we must address ourselves before we can accept this premise as the basis for all of our subsequent discussion and analysis. Is it possible that society and culture are merely projections of the individual? Will a knowledge of psychology enable us to account for social phenomena? From our discussion thus far it would seem clear that sociology cannot be reduced to psychology, but it is still necessary to examine the problem and to consider the relationship between individual and society.

Notes

[1] George Peter Murdock, "The Common Denominator of Cultures," in Ralph Linton (ed.), *The Science of Man in the World Crisis* (New York: Columbia University Press, 1945), p. 124.

[2] Clark Wissler, *Man and Culture* (New York: Crowell, 1923), p. 74.

[3] Robert S. Lynd and Helen M. Lynd, *Middletown* and *Middletown in Transition* (New York: Harcourt, 1929 and 1937).

[4] Samuel A. Stouffer *et al.*, *The American Soldier, II: Combat and Its Aftermath* (Princeton: Princeton University Press, 1949), 174.

[5] Clyde Kluckhohn, "Universal Categories of Culture," in Alfred L. Kroeber *et al.*, *Anthropology Today* (Chicago: University of Chicago Press, 1953), p. 513.

[6] See, for example, John W. Burgess, *Political Science and Comparative Constitutional Law,* I (Boston: Ginn, 1896), 37–9.

[7] Aristotle, *Politics,* trans. by William Ellis (London: Dent Everyman's Edition, 1912), p. 103.

[8] For a review of the development of racial categories until 1900 see Gustav Retzius, "The Development of Race Measurements and Classification," in Alfred L. Kroeber and Thomas T. Waterman (eds.), *Source Book in Anthropology* (rev. ed.; New York: Harcourt, 1931), pp. 94–102.

[9] Raymond Firth, *Human Types* (rev. ed.; New York: New American Library, 1958), p. 20.

[10] *Ibid.*

[11] *The Race Concept* (Paris: UNESCO, 1952), p. 11.

[12] Carleton S. Coon, with Edward E. Hunt, Jr., *The Living Races of Man* (New York: Knopf, 1965), pp. 9–10.

[13] See Margaret Mead, *Sex and Temperament in Three Primitive Societies* (New York: Morrow, 1935), Part I: "The Mountain-Dwelling Arapesh."

[14] Erich Fromm, "Sex and Character," in Ruth N. Anshen (ed.), *The Family: Its Function and Destiny* (New York: Harper, 1949), pp. 375–92.

[15] Betty Friedan, *The Feminine Mystique* (New York: Norton, 1963).

[16] Charles-Louis de Montesquieu, *The Spirit of Laws,* I, trans. by Thomas Nugent, rev. by J. V. Pritchard (New York: Appleton, 1900), pp. 315, 317–8.

[17] Griffith Taylor, *Urban Geography* (New York: Dutton, 1949).

[18] See Margaret Mead, *New Lives for Old* (New York: Morrow, 1956).

[19] *The New York Times,* July 23, 1957. The story described an attempt by the Air Force to test pills that would help men keep warm under Arctic conditions. It included the fact that researchers had some evidence that Negroes tended to chill more easily than whites, although the reasons for this difference were unclear.

[20] Émile Durkheim, *The Rules of Sociological Method,* trans. by Sarah A. Solovay and John H. Mueller (Chicago: University of Chicago Press, 1938), p. 102.

Suggestions for further reading

BIERSTEDT, ROBERT. *The Social Order.* Revised edition. New York: McGraw-Hill, 1963, Chs. 2, 3, 12.
A useful, well-written discussion in a recent textbook of the influence of geographical and biological factors on society. Chapter 10 examines the nature and source of differences between men and women.

COON, CARLETON S., WITH E. HUNT, JR. *The Living Races of Man.* New York: Knopf, 1965.
An effort to describe and account for the characteristics and distribution of races.

DUNN, L. C. AND THEODOSIUS DOBZHANSKY. *Heredity, Race, and Society.* New York: Penguin, 1946.
A brief analysis of individual and group differences in hereditary characteristics by two distinguished geneticists.

MEAD, MARGARET. *Male and Female.* New York: New American Library, 1955.
A full-scale attempt by a noted anthropologist to determine what is inherent and what is acquired in sexual roles and behavior.

MONTAGU, M. F. ASHLEY. *The Direction of Human Development.* New York: Harper, 1955.
A detailed examination of the biological bases of personality and social life. The author argues the innate goodness of human nature and attributes human flaws—moral and otherwise—to "human nurture."

MONTAGU, M. F. ASHLEY. *Man's Most Dangerous Myth: The Fallacy of Race.* New York: Columbia University Press, 1942.
A criticism of the concept of race as "An Ugly Human Error" and an examination of the relationship between group differences in physical characteristics and society and culture.

MURDOCK, GEORGE PETER. "The Common Denominator of Cultures," in Ralph Linton (ed.), *The Science of Man in the World Crisis*. New York: Columbia University Press, 1945, pp. 123–42. *An attempt to explain cultural universals by reference to the ways in which people learn.*

SERVICE, ELMAN R. *A Profile of Primitive Culture*. New York: Harper, 1958.
Brief summaries of the culture and social structure of twenty societies: primitive bands, tribes, "primitive states," and peasant communities. A useful review of the great variety found in human institutions, beliefs, and forms of organization.

4

culture, society, and the individual

Sociological and psychological perspectives

Human life, we have said, is group life. The isolated individual is a philosopher's fiction—Rousseau's "noble savage" and Hobbes's presocial man engaged in a perpetual war against others—or a tragic accident, as in the case of feral man. Men do not live apart, each seeking a private solution to the problems of survival. They live together, sharing a common way of life (a culture) that regulates their collective existence and provides methods for adapting to the world around them and for controlling and manipulating to some degree the forces of nature.

In viewing human experience from a sociological perspective which emphasizes the collective features of social life and the shared and patterned aspects of behavior, we seem to neglect the individual person. Sociologists study society and culture, social relationships and social norms, shared beliefs and common values, social structure and patterned behavior, as distinct from the individuals who conform to or deviate from social norms, subscribe to beliefs and values prevalent in their group, and participate in relationships embodied in social structures. Yet society and culture, as well as all the other abstractions we have used, do not, except in a metaphorical sense, live, behave, respond, adapt, adjust. Only individuals, alone or with others, act. All that we can observe is these individuals—who differ in some respects from one another—as they attend school, take marriage vows, look after children, work, vote, make political decisions, write books, go to church, and engage in the myriad other activities that make up a way of life. Culture and society become tangible only in the minds and actions of individuals.

Because the abstract character of sociological concepts and sociological analysis seems to contrast sharply with the concreteness of human behavior, it is necessary to consider the relationship between the individual and culture and society. The warrant for a point of view that seems to disregard the individual is both substantive and methodological; it lies not only in the nature of that relationship but also in the fact that it is possible to distinguish, for analytic purposes, between psychological and sociological aspects of behavior.

In its use of abstractions, sociology, as we noted earlier (see Chapter 1), is no different from other scientific disciplines. Psychology, which focuses upon the individual and his personality, also uses abstractions—ego, attitude, drive, stimulus, repression, learning, reinforcement—and psychological propositions are general statements about the relationships among variables. It is precisely the process of abstraction and the manipulation of the resulting ideas that constitute the core of any science.

Society and culture on the one hand and personality and the individual on the other are not sharply differentiated entities; they simply represent different conceptual foci for exploring the nature and sources of human behavior. Edward Sapir has graphically distinguished these alternative perspectives:

> If I see my little son playing marbles I do not, as a rule, wish to have light thrown on how the game is played. Nearly everything that I observe tends to be interpreted as a contribution to the understanding of the child's personality. He is bold or timid, alert or easily confused, a good sport or a bad sport when he loses, and so on. The game of marbles, in short, is merely an excuse, as it were, for the unfolding of various facts or theories about a particular individual's psychic constitution. But when I see a skilled laborer oiling a dynamo, or a polished mandarin seating himself at the dinner table in the capacity of academic guest, it is almost inevitable that my observations take the form of ethnographic field notes, the net result of which is likely to be facts or theories about such cultural patterns as the running of a dynamo or Chinese manners.[1]

The same item of behavior can thus be conceptualized from either a psychological or sociological point of view. Human conduct may be seen in relation to the structure and dynamics of the individual personality, or it may be viewed in relation to the organization and functioning of culture and society. The purchase of a mink coat, for example, may be looked upon as an action providing some kind of ego gratification for the buyer (or her husband), or as behavior contributing to the status of the woman (or her family). These perspectives are obviously those of psychology and sociology. They may be linked together, of course, in the observation that the buyer derives her ego gratification in part from the status she gains.

In conceptualizing the same phenomenon differently the sociologist and psychologist are led to ask different questions. Each approach enables us to explain some aspects of behavior; neither alone can explain the totality of behavior. The sociologist seeks to explain, for example, why the rate of alcoholism is low among Jews and high among Irish Catholics. The relevant questions would be: What are the differences in experience, values, attitudes, and social relationships that might be related to drinking? If one were to try to explain why any one individual—Jew or Irish Catholic—was an alcoholic, the answer would have to consider the structure of the personality, emotional stresses and tensions, and prior personal experience. Alcoholism can thus be considered as an affliction of an individual or as a patterned form of behavior occurring at a given rate in each group.

The distinctive perspectives and preoccupations of psychologist and sociologist have frequently led to distorted interpretations of human behavior against which each must guard. In his concern for the individual the psychologist has on occasion lost sight of the influence of social norms and social structure on personality. On the other hand the sociologist has sometimes reified such concepts as culture, society, institution, and role, transforming them from bloodless abstractions based on observation of repeated actions into concrete, active entities that presumably coerce individuals to ends or purposes distinct from those of living, acting, human beings.

Nor should the fact that it is both possible—and fruitful—to distinguish sociological and psychological perspectives from one another obscure the obvious interdependence of individual and society. Each person is simultaneously a carrier of culture, a participant in group life, and a distinctive personality—as well as a sentient biological organism. Personality is to a large extent a social product, while psychological traits are related in complex and subtle ways to culture and social structure.

The individual as a social product

Yet in a sense culture and society transcend the individual, for they are not dependent upon any specific person or persons in whose attitudes and actions they find expression. As Ralph Linton has observed:

> Unpleasant as the realization may be to egotists, very few individuals can be considered as more than incidents in the life histories of the societies to which they belong. Our species long ago reached the point where organized groups rather than their individual members became the functional units in its struggle for survival.[2]

Culture possesses an obvious continuity that extends beyond the lifetime of those who possess, create, and utilize it, and the structure of a society persists despite the continual replacement of its members.

Without society, the individual cannot survive. As we saw earlier, men possess no instinctive skills or knowledge, and no inherited patterns of behavior other than such automatic responses, or reflexes, as grasping, sucking, the knee jerk (*patellar*) response, blinking, and so on. The instruments with which men cope with their environment and organize their collective existence are derived from culture. Moreover, the infant requires not only the satisfaction of physical needs by others for a relatively long time, compared to other animals, but also their attention and care. This observation is hardly new; in the thirteenth century the Emperor Frederick II conducted an experiment that demonstrated the point clearly:

His second folly was that he wanted to find out what kind
of speech and what manner of speech children would have
when they grew up, if they spoke to no one beforehand. So
he bade foster mothers and nurses to suckle the children,
to bathe and wash them, but in no way to prattle with them
or to speak to them, for he wanted to learn whether they
would speak the Hebrew language, which was the oldest,
or Greek, or Latin, or Arabic, or perhaps the language of
their parents, of whom they had been born. But he laboured
in vain, because the children all died. For they could not
live without the petting and the joyful faces and loving
words of their foster mothers. And so the songs are called
"swaddling songs," which a woman sings while she is rocking
the cradle, to put a child to sleep, and without them a child
sleeps badly and has no rest.[3]

This conclusion has gained empirical support from
modern research, particularly studies by René Spitz, who
compared infants in a foundling home with children in an
isolated fishing village where physical conditions were difficult, with a group of middle-class infants, and particularly
with babies in a nursery attached to a penal institution for
delinquent girls.[4] In the foundling home nutritive, hygienic,
and medical care were good, but the children received little
personal attention from the nurses. (Each nurse, however
motherly she might be, could spend little time with one
child while responsible for eight.) In the penal institution,
physical conditions were equally adequate, but the children
were looked after much of the time by their mothers. The
conclusion drawn from comparison of these groups was that
the absence of "maternal care, maternal stimulation, and
maternal love" led not only to limited physical and emotional development, but also to a high mortality rate. Or,
in the words of a distinguished psychoanalyst, "Babies who
aren't loved don't live." [5] (This conclusion applies, however,
chiefly to the latter half of the first year of life.) Spitz's
specific findings have been challenged, chiefly on methodo-

logical grounds, but other research has generally sustained the verdict that "adequate 'mothering' or 'parenting' has vital significance for development." [6]

Each individual is born with a more or less distinctive physical equipment that will grow and mature. He enjoys a capacity for learning which distinguishes him from other animals. He has drives and needs—hunger and food, thirst and drink, libido (to use the Freudian term) and sexual gratification, as well as potentialities for emotional response —anger, fear, love, hate. But genetic traits and individual potentialities unfold and take on form only in the course of experience in a social environment. The individual learns to satisfy his needs in a socially approved fashion. What he eats and how often, whether he drinks cow's milk, goat's milk, or the fruit of the vine, whether he has a single sexual partner or many—all depend upon the culture. His likes and dislikes, hopes and ambitions, his interpretations of society itself and of the supernatural (if he comes to believe in the latter) are derived from the social world around him. In short, he becomes a social being as he absorbs a culture that enables him to survive and to live in society and that guides his actions and gives meaning to his existence.

Even such ostensibly "private" experiences as emotional response and perception are influenced by culture, as mediated through the activities of other persons with whom one interacts. In a perceptive study of hospital patients, for example, Mark Zborowski found that members of various ethnic groups responded very differently to the experience of physical pain. "Old Americans" tended to maintain a stoical attitude, although they might give way to crying or groaning—if no one was present—when the pain became acute. Both Jews and Italians, on the other hand, were likely to be "very emotional," complaining, groaning, moaning, or crying without any sense of shame. The Italian, however, when relieved by drugs "easily forgets his suf-

fering and manifests a happy and joyful disposition." The
Jew, on the other hand, remained concerned about the
source of his pain and often was reluctant to take analgesic
drugs for fear they might hide important symptoms.[7]

The influence of culture on perception may be illustrated
by the "moralistic story of the countryman and the cricket."

> Walking down a busy city street one day the countryman
> seized his city-bred friend by the arm, crying, "Listen to the
> chirp of the cricket!"
>
> The urbanite heard nothing until the bucolic friend led
> him to a crack in the face of a building where the cricket
> was proclaiming his presence unheard by the passing throngs.
>
> "How can you hear such a little sound in the midst of
> all this noise?" the city man wondered.
>
> "Watch," his friend replied as he tossed a dime upon the
> sidewalk. Whereupon a dozen people turned at the faint
> click of the coin.[8]

Sociological explanation and the individual

The close dependence of the individual upon his social
milieu makes it possible to account for some aspects of
human behavior without direct reference to psychological
characteristics. Since people tend to follow the norms of the
groups to which they belong, knowledge of an individual's
group affiliations and of the attributes of those groups is
likely to be sufficient to predict and account for his actions.
If one knows the social class of an Englishman, one can
predict quite accurately whether he will say "house" or
"home" when referring to his residence (the former is upper
class, the latter is not), or whether he will say "rich" or
"wealthy" when referring to his—or anyone else's—economic circumstances (the former is upper class, the latter
is not).[9] It is a safe prediction that middle-class Americans
—who may have very different personalities—have only

one wife; call their evening meal "dinner"; own a car, washing machine, dryer, and television set; and hope to send their children to college.

One can also assume that persons who have shared similar experiences and possess common social character- istics will behave, on the whole, in approximately the same fashion in the same situations, even when their behavior is not institutionally prescribed or when alternatives are left open to them by the culture. Because their values and per- spectives are alike, they tend to see the world and react to it in much the same way. If Americans share a common economic status, place of residence, and religious back- ground, for example, it is possible to predict, with a reason- able degree of reliability, how they will vote in national elections. (The degree of predictability is increased if one excludes the largely one-party South.)

The same explanatory model can help to account for variations in behavior. If one finds differences in language, dress, voting, eating habits, relations between parents and children, attitudes, beliefs, and so on, one need not explore the psychological attributes of each individual but can find an adequate explanation in the varied social experiences people have had and the contrasting norms and social structures of the groups to which they belong.

It must be understood, however, that the specific empir- ical conclusions which follow from these propositions are always statements of relative frequency or probability. Manual workers, on the whole, tend to think of themselves as belonging to the working class, but one nationwide study found that only 77 per cent of urban manual workers identified themselves in this fashion.[10] Most persons "swear" to perform their duties faithfully when they take an oath of public office in the United States, but a small number only "affirm" that they will do so. Or, to take a different type of finding, morale of industrial workers tends to be high when there are well-established work groups in the

factory; when workers have not established personal relationships with one another morale is likely to be low.[11]

These empirical findings are couched in statistical terms
in part because of the complexity of social life. Manual
workers possess, in addition to their occupations, many
other attributes that may influence their class identifications.
For example, those manual workers who do not consider
themselves members of the working class tend to have more
education and to come from white-collar families more
frequently than those who accept a working-class identification.[12] Those who "affirm" their responsibilities are Quakers whose religious beliefs keep them from "swearing" in a
conventional manner. Many other factors in addition to
relations with fellow workers may influence morale in the
factory; low wages or an unpleasant foreman can offset a
congenial group of co-workers, and an interesting job can
make up for the absence of pleasant social relationships.
As it is virtually impossible to take into account all the
social and cultural variables that affect human behavior,
there must always be some margin of error in sociological
analysis and prediction. In this, of course, sociology is not
peculiar, for all empirical research suffers, to a greater or
lesser degree, from the same disability.

The fact that the individual is largely a social product
and that it is therefore possible to account for many aspects
of his behavior by reference simply to culture and social
organization does not mean that he is merely a passive
instrument of his society. The relationship between society
and the individual is not that of puppeteer and puppet,
with the individual pulled hither and yon as the strings are
manipulated. "No anthropologist [or sociologist]," wrote
Ruth Benedict, "with a background of experience of other
cultures has ever believed that individuals were automatons,
mechanically carrying out the decrees of their civilization." [13] The individual is not merely a tape recording of his
culture, if we may shift the metaphor, even if he sometimes

plays back parts of the recording as various occasions require. He must be seen as an active being who is likely to behave in a more or less standardized fashion, but who also possesses the capacity for innovation and deviation and may through his actions significantly influence and change the nature of his culture and society.

The tendency to conform to cultural requirements and social expectations cannot be seen as "normal," but must be taken as problematical; it is not something to be assumed, but a fact to be explained. We need to explore, therefore, the process by which the organism becomes a person capable of participating actively in the life of society and to examine the relevance of personality and psychological dynamics for the structure and functioning of society.

Agencies of socialization

The process of *socialization,* which transforms the raw human material into a social being, serves two major functions. On the one hand, it prepares the individual for the roles he is to play, providing him with the necessary repertoire of habits, beliefs, and values, the appropriate patterns of emotional response and modes of perception, the requisite skills and knowledge. On the other hand, by communicating the contents of the culture from one generation to the other, it provides for its persistence and continuity.

The chief agency in this process is usually the family or kinship group. In ministering to the needs of the helpless infant, the parents—initially, in most cases, the mother— establish a relationship with him that is of central importance in his future development. The child discovers how to secure satisfaction of his bodily requirements by communicating, through sound and gestures, with others. First as a largely passive member of the family and then more actively, he learns to play appropriate roles and acquires the abilities, attitudes, and modes of response that enable him to participate in social life outside the family circle. Because one's earliest and closest ties are usually with parents, siblings, and sometimes other kinfolk, family experience and expectations carry a special emotional weight and are therefore of particular importance in shaping personality and transmitting cultural demands and expectations.

Everywhere, however, there are also other persons or groups that participate in the socialization process. Occasionally other agencies may almost replace the family. The Israeli kibbutz, for example, assigns care of small children to a communal nursery, except for the few hours each day that they spend with their parents. When children are old enough to leave the nursery they still remain with their age-mates in a communal setting rather than with their families. Peer groups, in fact, are found in most societies, and in some they serve important functions in defining appropriate behavior, setting standards, and inculcating goals. Through various institutionalized sanctions they may also enforce conformity to established norms, including those specific to their age group.

In contrast with the family, which is typically more authoritarian (and, from the child's viewpoint always so in some degree) and more likely to transmit traditional values, the peer group usually offers a more egalitarian experience, although it too may on occasion become rigidly authoritarian in its demands upon its members. Within the peer group there are often opportunities to explore topics tabooed in relations with adults, and to secure support from others as young people seek to break away from parental constraints and establish an independent identity.

The family alone cannot adequately train children for many adult roles in a complex industrial society, and other agencies, particularly the school, therefore also contribute significantly to preparation for adult life. Not only is the school expected to transmit skills and practical knowledge, but important cultural values as well: patriotism, ambition, concern for others, and so on. The impact of the school is affected, of course, by family attitudes and behavior, which can facilitate formal educational efforts or impede them. The school itself includes both the formal organization, with prepared curriculum and established procedures, and the teachers, with whom students can establish personal relationships that may significantly affect their attitudes and behavior. It also provides a convenient center for the development of informal, though often important, peer groups.

Finally, in contemporary society, the mass media contribute to the socialization of the child—and the continuing socialization of the adult. In the information they make available, the models of behavior they provide, the values they express and illustrate, the experiences—vicarious thrills, entertainment, horror, and so on—they offer, the mass media can reinforce the efforts of family and school, or weaken and dilute them. Children can learn directly from the media, which also communicate to parents and peers standards of behavior they then transmit. The media may be deliberately utilized for education and indoctrination, as in educational television in the United States or in the exploitation of all forms of mass communication in authoritarian societies where the regimes systematically try to spread and sustain the values that they approve.

In a complex and heterogeneous society lacking "official" values and with no central direction and control, the influence of the mass media is usually unplanned and uncertain, potentially dysfunctional in relation to prevailing standards of some groups, or to those of the whole society. Even in a totalitarian society, there may be a gap between intention and result, with unanticipated and unwanted consequences flowing from both the content and the techniques of the media.

Unlike a traditional and relatively stable society in which the agencies of socialization are limited and tend to function together harmoniously, a complex modern society subjects the individual to a diverse array of socializing influences that are not likely to be consistent with one another. The child hears in Sunday School that "the meek shall inherit the earth," but he may also witness admiration for the strong and powerful on the part of his parents and in the mass media. The eleven-year-old whose parents are reluctant to discuss "the facts of life" may see a photograph of an unborn foetus on the cover of *Life Magazine* and be able to read a detailed, fully illustrated account of its development. The expectations of parents and peer groups often conflict, and the schools may demand more—or less —from the child or young adult than his parents have prepared him for. (The contemporary unwillingness of American college and university administrators to serve *in loco parentis,* in part because of student pressure, creates difficulties for some students not yet ready for a fully independent adult role.)

The consequences of such inconsistency are complicated and varied. On the one hand the individual may find himself uncertain and ill-prepared for playing the roles expected of him, or even, in some instances, with serious internal conflicts. On the other hand, as he learns to cope with diverse influences and pressures, he may become more autonomous, that is, more capable of making independent judgments about the desirability of conforming to cultural norms. The conditions that determine the outcome have yet to be adequately delineated.

In a changing society, both the techniques for training a child and the substance of that training usually combine the new and the traditional. Mothers may rely upon what their mothers told them and also upon the latest advice from the child-care specialist. The schools seek to inculcate and reinforce many of the traditional moral verities while teaching new skills and exploiting modern techniques. To some extent parents and teachers inevitably express in the methods they use a carry-over from their own earlier experience at the same time that they are responding to the changes that have taken place in the world in which they live.

The socializing agencies themselves are continually subject to external forces that affect their socializing function. Modern science, communicated through the schools and the mass media, has influenced the ways in which parents look after their children, take care of their needs, and respond to their behavior. Governmental bodies impose controls over the contents of the mass media and governmental programs determine the resources available to the schools. For families that are unable to provide adequately for their children, for either economic or psychological reasons, there may be aid and support from welfare agencies of various kinds. A changing economic order and expanding technology lead to changes in the schools and to a redefinition of the qualities encouraged in children as prerequisites for success.

The process of socialization

Socialization is a complex and multifaceted process. As he grows, each individual's biological impulses are directed into culturally patterned channels. Appropriate responses are "reinforced," inappropriate ones "extinguished" by a system of rewards and punishments. He learns which gestures or actions elicit food, cuddling, or elimination of discomfort, and how he is expected to respond to the actions of others. Eventually, he comes to eat three meals each day rather than two, to handle food with implements rather than stuffing it into his mouth with his fingers, to perform his bodily functions at the appropriate time and in the appropriate place. Much of this learning, then, consists of the development of habits that cónform to the customs of the society.

The channeling of drives and the acquisition of acceptable habits are not a mechanical process but are linked with judgments of right and wrong, good and bad. One not only learns to do something in a particular way, but also that it is the right or correct way. Values, which reinforce and sustain many habits, are learned chiefly from parents, sometimes didactically through direct instruction, in part through expressions of approval or disapproval for conformity or nonconformity. A middle-class child in the United States who takes something that does not belong to him is told to "give it back," and is informed that one does not take another's property. If he fails to complete some assigned task—homework, mowing the lawn, piano or violin practice—he will be reminded of the importance of persistence and of doing things well. Slovenliness, carelessness, and procrastination are criticized in middle-class homes, whereas neatness, precision, and doing chores on time are rewarded. In other societies, of course, and to some extent in other social classes, different values and standards are encouraged. For example, modesty, usually stressed in American families, is relatively unimportant among the Trobriand Islanders; respect for elders, traditionally strongly emphasized among the British middle and upper classes, is much less emphatically stressed in the United States; equality, a major American value, is much less important in most Western European societies.

Children acquire values—and attitudes and beliefs—not only through explicit precept and overt reward or punishment, but also through suggestion, implication, and example. Nothing need be said explicitly for the child to recognize qualities that are valued highly and those that are not. Sensitive to emotional nuances in parental behavior, he can often recognize implicit approval or disapproval of his own or someone else's actions even when it is not openly expressed. Models for conventional (or unconventional) forms of behavior are found in the mass media and among peers as well as in the family.

The individual, however, is more than a mere bundle of habits and values, attitudes and beliefs, all of them learned and culturally patterned. This bundle of psychological elements is organized into a structure, the "personality," in which the parts are related to one another and not randomly organized. A personality, therefore, possesses attributes that render it more than the mere sum of its parts.

The term *personality* is difficult to define and is as variously used as *society*—perhaps even more so. Yet most psychologists would agree, no matter how they use the term, that it refers to some kind of psychological structure or organization. They disagree among themselves about what elements constitute the personality and the mechanisms through which the psychological system functions.[14]

Of central importance in personality is the *self,* the individual's awareness of and feeling about his own personal and social identity. The self serves an integrating function for the personality; the significance of habits, attitudes, values, and beliefs depend largely upon their relationship to one's feelings about one's self. One responds more readily and more intensely to those external events that impinge upon one's self-image and self-evaluations than to those in which one's self is not involved. The participant in a group conversation pricks up his ears at a vaguely heard reference to himself from a distant corner, though he "hears" nothing else. He remains calm and objective as various topics are discussed, only rising angrily—or pleasantly—at comments which might be taken as referring to *his* personality, *his* relations to others.

Our understanding of the nature, origins, and functions of the self and its relations to social life rests to a large extent upon the contributions of Charles Horton Cooley, an economist turned sociologist and one of America's seminal sociological theorists, and George Herbert Mead, Cooley's contemporary and a philosopher and social psychologist.

Building upon earlier work by William James and the psychologist James M. Baldwin, Cooley emphasized the interdependence of self and society. Although he felt that "the emotion or feeling of self may be regarded as an instinct" (a view not shared by many other students of personality), it was only "defined and developed by experience." [15] The most significant types of experience, he asserted, took place within "primary groups": family, play group, and neighborhood. Necessarily a member of these groups during childhood, the most plastic period of his development, the individual acquires basic human characteristics and sentiments within them. These groups were "primary" because they were "fundamental in forming the social nature and ideas of the individual"; they were "the nursery of human nature." [16]

Through the medium of language, which is obviously social in character, the individual derives the ideas that he adopts as his own. The attitude one takes toward one's own character—physical, psychological, and social—is significantly affected by the attitudes of others. If they approve of his actions or appearance, or he thinks they do, then he too approves of them, and vice versa. Cooley called this self-image the "looking-glass self," which, he said, "seems to have three principal elements: the imagination of our appearance to the other person; the imagination of his judgment of that appearance; and some sort of self-feeling, such as pride or mortification." [17]

Mead's contribution, which he and many other scholars

viewed as an extension and elaboration of Cooley's analysis, also focuses upon the self as a social product.

> The self [he wrote] has a character which is different from that of the physiological organism proper. The self is something which has a development; it is not initially there, at birth, but arises in the process of social experience and activity, that is, develops in the given individual as a result of his relations to that process as a whole and to other individuals within that process.[18]

The distinctive quality of the self is that "it is an object to itself"; it can achieve distance and objectivity of some sort in looking at and evaluating itself.

Through language and gestures the individual learns to put himself in the place of others and to act as they might— to play their roles. By continually doing so he develops the capacity to look at himself from their standpoint and comes to orient his behavior to the expectations of others, both directly and through the points of view he has *internalized,* that is, incorporated into his own personality.

> The individual experiences himself as such, not directly, but only indirectly, from the particular standpoints of other individual members of the same group, or from the generalized standpoint of the social group as a whole to which he belongs.[19]

Mead's work was largely speculative, based upon his observations of his own behavior and of others around him and upon his study of philosophical and psychological literature. Yet similar conclusions have also been derived from careful empirical research. On the basis of a careful and painstaking study of children, for example, Jean Piaget, the distinguished Swiss social psychologist, concluded that

"Social life is necessary if the individual is to become conscious of his own mind." [20]

While Cooley and Mead saw clearly the extent to which the self was a social product and emphasized the importance of language and communication, Sigmund Freud, the founder of psychoanalysis and the most influential student of human behavior of the past century, stressed the emotional dynamics of socialization and personality development. Despite a strong belief in the instinctive and unchanging nature of human drives, Freud saw in family relationships a crucial factor in the formation of personality. Although he largely ignored the institutional character of the family, he examined in great and perceptive detail the complex interaction of mother, father, and children, and the psychological consequences of these relationships. From his analysis came significant additions to our knowledge of both personality dynamics and the processes by which people come to follow—or to ignore—the dictates of society.

Emerging from the interaction between parents and children, according to Freud, are emotional attachments that contribute in strategic ways to the personality. Because of the intimacy and emotional ties, children tend to *identify* with their parents, to want to become as much like them as possible. Sons are apt to identify with their fathers, daughters with their mothers, although the process is sometimes only partially completed, sometimes never, and sometimes takes unusual or distorted forms. Eventually the standards of the parents—which are usually also the standards of the society—become part of the child's personality, an internalized guardian that watches over and judges his actions. This "introjected" or internalized parent—the parental image which becomes part of the child's personality—Freud called the *superego*. One of the latter's functions, he pointed out, is to serve as "the vehicle of tradition and of all the age-long values which have been handed down . . . from generation to generation." [21] In a sense, the parent is always present and failure to live up to parental standards can generate a more or less painful sense of guilt, for these internalized norms constitute the conscience. (Like Mead, Freud also noted that "the ego can take itself as an object, it can treat itself like any other object, observe itself, criticize itself, and do Heaven knows what besides with itself." [22] One may, of course, for various reasons fail to obey these rules and suffer the pangs of guilt, but in most instances, it would appear, the fear of guilt serves to induce conformity to those social norms embodied in parental precepts.

In addition to those values in terms of which the person judges his self, or ego, the superego incorporates goals and conceptions of achievement which the individual strives to realize—in Freudian terms, the *ego-ideal*. In seeking to be like the parent and to live up to his expectations, now internalized and part of the personality, the individual is driven to pursue socially approved goals. Thus, unless his model or mentor is himself a criminal, rebel, or eccentric, the individual learns to want what the culture says he should want—to become rich and famous, to perform some socially valued tasks, to be a respectable and law-abiding citizen. Goals and ideals, then, as well as norms and moral standards, derive from the social and psychological interaction between parents or parent-substitutes and the child. The person is not simply hedged about with internalized restrictions or coerced into required modes of behavior by his conscience, but also acquires the springs of action that can channel impulses and energies into lines of effort that are potentially both socially useful and personally gratifying.

This highly generalized process of personality development is subject, of course, to endless variations. Families are broken and the usual sequence cannot take place. Other adults replace parents, who may be rejected by their own children. In a society in which all children are looked after by women, the son's initial attachment to his mother may

be so strong that he finds it difficult to establish a close
relationship with his father and to identify with him. For
various reasons, the son may remain closely attached to his
mother and the daughter to the father. In these varied circumstances, the child may never come to internalize the
values of the culture or may not assign to particular values
and goals the same importance they assume for others. Alternatively, he may acquire values or psychological tendencies appropriate to the prevailing social and cultural
demands through these less typical sequences; as Warner
and Abegglen point out, for example, many mobile business
executives appear to lack strong attachments to their fathers
but are deeply influenced by their mothers.[23] If there are
differences in family structure, relatives other than either
father or mother may play a central role in personality
development.[24]

Finally, some of the components of personality that
affect social action and that may, indeed, be of considerable
importance in determining how men play various social
roles derive from the methods of child care and child training. Psychoanalytically oriented scholars have tried to
demonstrate a relationship between how children are fed,
toilet trained, and disciplined, on the one hand, and various
institutions, beliefs, and values on the other.[25] Although
there seems to be little conclusive evidence of a direct connection between child-rearing techniques and specific patterns of behavior, general personality traits do appear to be
significantly affected by how children are looked after and
trained.

The type of discipline imposed upon the child, for example, generates an attitude toward authority in general
that may be important in shaping adult response to the
exercise of authority. Children brought up in rigid, authoritarian families without a great deal of warmth and affection,
it has been argued on the basis of at least some empirical
evidence, tend to become rigid personalities who are sub-

missive toward constituted authority and at the same time delight in ordering others about.[26] (Under some circumstances, however, these "authoritarian personalities" revolt violently because their own feelings are in fact deeply ambivalent, and their ready acceptance of authority conceals a deep hostility toward and resentment against the rigid discipline to which they were once subject.) Other important personality traits—aggressiveness, restraint, competitiveness, distrust, acceptance—also reflect not simply the explicit values of the culture, but the modes of child-rearing as well.

Adult socialization: continuities and discontinuities

Although there is now general agreement that the most important elements in socialization take place during childhood, there is no point at which one can say that the process is complete. As the individual matures he enters—or passes through—new roles, each with its own requirements. Many of these roles build upon the physical capacities that come with maturation—adolescence, motherhood, military service—and upon the skills, knowledge, values, and motivations gained earlier. The child starts school only when he has reached an age at which society feels that his physical, social, and intellectual skills will enable him to cope with the new demands made upon him—at five in England, six in the United States (if one ignores nursery school and kindergarten), and seven in the Soviet Union. He enters the occupational world after he has acquired at least some of the prerequisites for employment or has undergone the training needed for a specific job.

Part of the preparation for many adult roles consists not only in learning necessary skills, but also in instilling appropriate motivations and values. Unlike Peter Pan, most children want to grow up and become parents, workers, soldiers, citizens. They are ready to make the effort necessary to learn how to play these roles and have often already incorporated the values linked with them. Under such conditions, that is, where there has been "anticipatory socialization," learning proceeds easily and effectively.

Adult roles, however, on occasion do not rest upon motivations, values, and abilities already acquired, and childhood experience provides little preparation for what is expected later. Among the Manus of New Guinea, for example, boys are free and unrestrained, bearing little responsibility and subject to little or no authority. Yet upon maturity they are suddenly thrust into a complex system of debts, obligations, and responsibilities which they are expected—and forced—to accept.[27] Such discontinuities might be expected to produce strain and tension, perhaps even efforts to escape from new demands being made. Yet acceptance of the role is often rapid because of the pressures brought to bear by others and the absence of a significant group upon which the individual can call for support in resisting the new role requirements.

In a complex and changing society there are perhaps inescapable discontinuities in the successive roles that people learn to play. Because of the diversity of occupational roles, for example, the ability of parents and schools to prepare people adequately for the tasks they will perform and the problems they will face is limited, and the process of socialization must therefore continue through adult life. Rapid social change requires new patterns of behavior and difficult emotional adjustments that could hardly have been anticipated. Whites who have always thought Negroes inferior must learn to accept them as equals as patterns of race relations change. Men who grow up with fixed ideas as to masculine superiority may have to learn to accept orders from women superiors as barriers to the advancement of women are lowered and more of them pursue professional careers. The solitary scholar may have to accommodate himself to organized research programs and the worker whose know-how is replaced by modern technology must acquire new skills.

Educational institutions, the mass media, and peer groups continue to serve as agencies of socialization for adults, supplemented by the complex organizations in which people carry on many of their activities. Within these organizations efforts are made not only to familiarize the newcomer to established routines but also to inculcate the particular values and loyalties that maintain the structure and lead to conformity to the demands of the new role. These efforts involve explicit instruction, the promise of rewards for conformity and penalties for nonconformity, and the give-and-take of personal interaction with others who express the values and expectations of the organization.[28]

The potentialities for adult socialization, however, may be limited as a result of prior experience. Early social relationships and the events of childhood have lasting effects upon personality, as Freud so clearly showed, and upon the individual's capacity to adapt to changing circumstances and learn new ways. Children who are allowed to express their feelings—including hostility and violence—freely and openly may find it difficult in later life to exercise emotional restraint. Thus lower-class children who come from an emotionally unconstrained background often are not able to take on readily the restraint characteristic of the middle class that is expected of them in school and later on the job.

The lasting effects of early socialization should not be overemphasized, though there is continuing disagreement as to just how persistent they are. There are institutions such as mental hospitals, welfare agencies, courts, and prisons that are intended to secure major changes in values, personality, and the ability to cope with social situations. Whenever the individual can be removed from familiar social contexts, the possibility of *resocialization*—major changes in personality and values—is increased, as cases of political "brainwashing" in various countries reveal.

(There is some evidence, however, that return to familiar
routines tends to restore the older patterns of thought,
feeling, and action.)

Without minimizing the relevance of the basic personality attributes established in early childhood, it is necessary
to remember that the individual is engaged in an ongoing
social process. He is always a "focus of group affiliations" [29]
that entail various expectations concerning behavior and
are enforced by diverse social sanctions. His response to
these social requirements and the persons with whom he
comes into contact will be affected by the personal characteristics he brings to the situation, though his personality
may in turn be changed in various ways by his new experiences.

Social character and social structure

Because the individual is to such a large extent a product
of his social experience, those who have been brought up
in the same fashion can be expected to be much like one
another and to differ from those reared under another
regimen. Culture not only provides the values and attitudes
transmitted to children but also defines the patterns of
child-rearing that affect the structure and dynamics of the
personality.[30] The psychological traits common to those
who have been socialized in the same fashion constitute a
"social character" which is potentially related in diverse
ways to values and beliefs as well as the institutionalized
system of social relationships.

Efforts to generalize about the character of social groups
is not new. Aristotle, for example, compared the "Asiatics,
whose understandings are quick and who are conversant in
the arts, [but] are deficient in courage; and therefore are
always conquered and the slaves of others" with the Greeks,
who were "both courageous and sensible," and therefore

"free, and governed in the best manner possible." [31] In recent times the question of "national character" has been dealt with in diverse fashion by historians, novelists, and others. Leo Tolstoy once characterized various Europeans as follows:

> Germans are self-confident on the basis of an abstract notion —science, that is, the supposed knowledge of absolute truth. A Frenchman is self-assured because he regards himself personally, both in mind and body, as irresistibly attractive to men and women. An Englishman is self-assured, as being a citizen of the best-organized state in the world, and there-fore as an Englishman always knows that all he does as an Englishman is undoubtedly correct. An Italian is self-assured because he is excitable and easily forgets himself and other people. A Russian is self-assured because he knows nothing and does not want to know anything, since he does not believe that anything can be known.[32]

(Tolstoy's generalizations can, of course, be challenged, yet with characteristic acuity, he focused upon an important psychological attribute, the basis for self-evaluation.) In a perceptive account of the Russians, a contemporary British writer observed:

> The average Russian can be plunged for long periods into moods of either pessimism or optimism, either apathy or concentrated efforts, and under the stimulus of persons around him he can also change his moods rapidly and show that they are changed, yet he cannot be called volatile or superficial. . . . [There is also] the well known tendency of many Russians to break out, at long intervals, into wild outbursts of joy or grief, anger, drunkenness, cruelty.[33]

Although generalizations about national character are often couched in stereotyped terms that ignore both the range of variation and the existence of individual differences, they cannot be casually dismissed. There is little doubt, despite great differences within a nation, that Englishmen and Americans, Russians and Frenchmen, Cubans and Chinese do differ from one another not only culturally, but also psychologically—in self-conceptions, modes of response, definitions of masculinity and femininity, attitudes toward sex, and so on. Our knowledge of the character, extent, and consequences of such differences is as yet crude and often inadequate, although the theories and methods needed to enlarge our understanding are steadily developing.[34]

National traits and the differences among members of various societies and social groups have been variously attributed to race, climate, geography, and history. We have already noted the inadequacies of a racial explanation of group similarities and differences and the limitations of climatic and geographic interpretations (see Chapter 3), although weather and the physical habitat obviously can enter into the experiences that affect personality. The impact of history, while unquestioned, must be precisely defined; it may refer to awareness of and reverence for the past as such, to traditions derived from earlier times and carried down through the generations, to those institutions shaped in the past that define how children shall be looked after and what they shall be taught.

Our growing understanding of the agencies and processes of socialization now makes it possible to explore more systematically the relationship between social character and specific institutions and social structures. A number of studies, chiefly of small, relatively homogeneous communities, have tried to identify the type of social character produced by particular methods of socialization and to relate it to specific values, beliefs, and forms of social organization. A detailed analysis of the people of Alor, a small island in what is now Indonesia, for example, found that mothers, busily at work in the fields, tended to neglect their children, who characteristically developed into anxious and suspicious adults ready to participate in a harsh, competitive society. Their religion and folklore also revealed distrust and uncertainty, which might both reflect the basic personality structure and contribute to its formation.[35]

The close link between personality and culture found in communities such as Alor and the high degree of consistency between them are not paralleled in larger, more complex societies in which methods of child-rearing are more varied, the influences to which children are exposed more diverse, and the roles open to individuals more numerous and more differentiated. Rather than a single "social character" there may be several, or many. Distinctive methods of socialization among subgroups—the middle class, Negroes, and Jews, for example—may generate identifiable character or personality types. In a multigroup society there may be both values that become part of the personalities of most people and psychological attributes peculiar to members of particular groups. Despite some systematic inquiry and a good deal of speculation, the psychological dimensions of a complex society have yet to be adequately delineated.

Even without a clear-cut definition of social character it is possible to identify psychological traits that affect patterns of response in social situations. Some of these traits— emotional needs, drives, feelings, orientations to others—are clearly related to the process of socialization. In a perceptive and influential analysis of American character, David Riesman focused upon changing "modes of conformity," those "components of personality that . . . play the principal role in the maintenance of social forms." [36] A major study by Adorno, Frenkel-Brunswik, Levinson, and Sanford examined in great detail the sources of the "authoritarian personality" and its relationship to prejudice.[37] Other psychological attributes are products of the culture and social structure within which individuals carry on their daily lives. In a study of a one-day radio campaign by Kate Smith

during World War II in which she sold $39 million worth
of war bonds, it was found that one reason for her success
was her apparent sincerity. It was this quality that appealed
to people who, because of their position in American society, felt a "craving for reassurance, an acute need to believe, a flight into faith." [38]

As these studies of the authoritarian personality and
mass persuasion suggest, psychological characteristics generated by social experience are important not only because
they account for conformity to social norms and group
expectations, but also because they enter in various ways
into the dynamics of the social system and, frequently, into
the process of social change. It has been pointed out, for
example, that American culture encourages feelings of guilt
and self-blame among those who do not achieve economic
success, because it assigns to each individual the full responsibility for his own economic fate. These feelings in
turn serve a significant social function for they focus criticism upon the individual rather than upon those institutions and social structures which make success difficult for
members of some groups to achieve.[39]

By repressing men's desires and enforcing modes of behavior which run counter to impulses and drives, both
innate and acquired, the process of socialization and the
demands society frequently makes of its members create
psychological problems for society. One of Freud's chief contributions to our understanding of the dynamics of personality is his demonstration of an inevitable degree of tension
between inherited impulses and drives of the organism and
the requirements of social life. It is possible to accept the
conclusion that men pay a psychological price for the acquisition of culture without accepting Freud's theory that
culture is merely the product of sublimated sexual urges, a
reward for renouncing instinctual gratification or a substitute for such gratification. The organism is constrained by
its social experience in manifold ways; the individual must

learn to control at least some of his impulses and to channel his drives along accepted lines.

The very nature of the social process itself adds to the inevitable tension between individual and society. No society is so fully integrated that the individual is free from uncertainty and conflicting demands. Sentiments or feelings generated by social life often must be restrained or inhibited. Demands for novelty or excitement are unfulfilled in a routine and unchanging way of life. Sacrifices may be required for the welfare of others without regard to personal wishes. *"Dulce et decorum est pro patria mori,"* Linton has noted, "expresses the social point of view. The individual who has to do the dying may acquiesce in its propriety, but it can hardly seem sweet to him." [40]

One significant aspect of culture and social structure, therefore, is the way in which they deal with the emotional needs of individuals. "If society is to survive," Linton observes, "culture must not only provide techniques for training and repressing the individual, it must also provide him with compensations and outlets. If it thwarts and suppresses him in certain directions, it must help him to expand in others . . . [and] must also provide the individual with harmless outlets for his socially repressed desires." [41] Failure to do these things will stimulate both deviation from social norms and social change.

Individual differences

That individuals resemble one another because of their social backgrounds or even that they possess common psychological attributes does not mean that individuals do not differ—often greatly—from one another. Indeed, differences among individuals persist for many reasons—biological, psychological, and sociological. Socialization produces people capable of playing social roles; it does not lead to identical personalities indistinguishable from one another.

Man is not a *tabula rasa* upon which culture writes; nor, to change the figure, is he a lump of clay to be molded by society. The unique biological equipment that each person possesses necessarily enters into the formation of his personality, which is not simply the sum derived from the addition of culture to organism but a result of a complex interaction between individual and society. What is sometimes called temperament, for example, that is, the generalized mode of response—rapid or slow, phlegmatic or lively —seems to be essentially inherited and closely related to biological functioning. "No culture yet observed," Ruth Benedict has commented, "has been able to eradicate the differences in the temperaments of the persons who compose it." [42]

No single individual incorporates in his personality the whole of his culture, or even all of those segments of it that enter into his experience. The middle-class American child is hardly likely to be exposed to the same cultural patterns or social experience as the child of a steelworker or a Hollywood movie star. Although they may all see the same television programs and read some of the same books, the specific content of each is interpreted differently, at least in some degree, and has somewhat different consequences.

Even though the socialization process is roughly similar for those in comparable social circumstances, it inevitably differs in individual cases in subtle, yet often important details. Insofar as the self emerges out of interaction with a limited number of other people, its character will reflect the idiosyncratic attributes they possess. The composition of the family or household, the complex interaction among parents, the specific events that occur during the impressionable years of childhood, and many chance factors contribute to the characteristics that distinguish each individual from others.

Adherence to the same social norm, therefore, does not necessarily carry the same emotional weight for each person. The child may be forced to remain clean at a very early age or he may gradually and easily learn that it is considered better to be clean than dirty. In each case he has learned the social norm, but the emotional concomitants are not likely to be the same. Any element derived from the culture may therefore have various functions in the psychic economy of individuals.

These distinctive personality attributes affect individual responses to the prescriptions of the culture and the expectations and demands of others. Temperamental variations, for example, can affect the reaction to the culture in which individuals happen to be born. A phlegmatic person in a strenuous, fast-moving society will respond quite differently from a lively, active one; the roles he will choose (when he has a choice), and how he performs required social roles may well be affected by his temperamental characteristics. Suggestible persons may readily be persuaded by the latest television commercial while others remain unmoved; aggressive children participate readily in some kinds of games while shy ones seek other activities. Out of these complex modes of response emerges patterns of behavior the explanation for which must inevitably include the psychological traits of individuals, although the sociologist relates these traits to the facts of social organization rather than to the structure or functioning of the individual personality.

Postscript

The problem with which this chapter has dealt, the relations between individual and society, clearly is of interest not only to social scientists. It is a persistent question which has also preoccupied men throughout human history, from the earliest philosophers and religious leaders to present-day scholars and moralists, for the answer inevitably possesses moral and political implications. It is a question of particular relevance in the modern world, where large-scale organization and totalitarian regimes threaten ruthlessly to subordinate the individuals to group purposes and to control and manipulate his daily activities, his beliefs and attitudes, and even his conception of himself, without that respect for the individual which constitutes one of the richest strands in the Western cultural tradition. The contemporary cultural themes of alienation, anomie, and disenchantment so prevalent in literature, philosophy, and theology, as well as in social science, focus upon the individual's relations to his society and the forces that limit his freedom.

We cannot explore the many answers that have been given to these questions in the past or their implications. To do so would lead us into problems of intellectual history and the sociology of ideas and knowledge. The lessons of modern social science concerning the interdependence of individual and society, however, can make some contribution to our understanding of the moral and political issues inherent in the continuing discussion and debate about the possibilities of individual freedom and the extent of the individual's dependence upon and subordination to the society in which he lives.

Although sociological analysis focuses upon the available reliable knowledge, the student must continually remind himself that theoretical controversies and empirical findings have a wider than scientific import, and that sociology, like any other human activity, cannot be extracted from its social context. The student of society must try to disassociate himself from the values of his society in his scientific endeavors, but nevertheless he can hardly forget that he is a member of society and that his findings and conclusions have social consequences.

Notes

[1] David Mandelbaum (ed.), *Selected Writings of Edward Sapir* (Berkeley: University of California Press, 1949), p. 590.

[2] Ralph Linton, *The Cultural Background of Personality* (New York: Appleton, 1945), p. 12.

[3] James B. Ross and Mary M. McLaughlin (eds.), *The Portable Medieval Reader* (New York: Viking, 1949), pp. 366–7.

[4] René A. Spitz, "Hospitalism: An Inquiry Into the Genesis of Psychiatric Conditions in Early Childhood," *Psychoanalytic Study of the Child*, I (1945), 53–74; and René A. Spitz, "Hospitalism: A Follow-up Report," *Psychoanalytic Study of the Child*, II (1946), 113–7.

[5] Sandor Ferenczi, quoted in Linton, *op. cit.*, p. 9.

[6] L. Joseph Stone and Joseph Church, *Childhood and Adolescence* (New York: Random House, 1957), p. 63. See pp. 58–66 for a review of the literature on this problem.

[7] Mark Zborowski, "Cultural Components in Responses to Pain," *Journal of Social Issues*, IV (1952), pp. 16–30.

[8] E. Adamson Hoebel, "The Nature of Culture," in Harry L. Shapiro (ed.), *Man, Culture, and Society* (New York: Oxford, 1956), pp. 175–6.

[9] These examples are drawn from Nancy Mitford (ed.), *Noblesse Oblige* (New York: Harper, 1956). A comparable, though much briefer, list of class differences in the use of language in the United States is offered in E. Digby Baltzell, *Philadelphia Gentlemen* (New York: Free Press, 1958), p. 51. Baltzell's list is much shorter, in part because he does not attempt the elaborate exploration reported in Mitford, in part because class differences in language are not so great in the United States as in England.

[10] Richard Centers, *The Psychology of Social Classes* (Princeton: Princeton University Press, 1949), p. 86.

[11] See Elton Mayo and G. F. F. Lombard, *Teamwork and Turnover in the Aircraft Industry of Southern California* (Boston:

Harvard Business School, 1944); and Elliott Jacques, *The Changing Culture of a Factory* (New York: Dryden, 1952).

[12] Centers, *op. cit.*, Table 68, p. 164, and Table 77, p. 180.

[13] Ruth Benedict, *Patterns of Culture* (New York: Pelican, 1946), p. 234.

[14] See Calvin Hall and Gardner Lindzey, *Theories of Personality* (New York: Wiley, 1957).

[15] Charles H. Cooley, *Human Nature and the Social Order* (New York: Scribner, 1902), p. 139.

[16] Charles H. Cooley, *Social Organization* (New York: Scribner, 1929; originally published in 1909), p. 23.

[17] Cooley, *Human Nature and the Social Order*, p. 152.

[18] George Herbert Mead, *Mind, Self, and Society* (Chicago: University of Chicago Press, 1934), p. 135.

[19] *Ibid.*, p. 138.

[20] Jean Piaget, *The Moral Judgment of the Child*, trans. by Marjorie Gabain (New York: Free Press, 1948), p. 407.

[21] Sigmund Freud, *New Introductory Lectures on Psycho-analysis*, trans. by W. J. H. Sprott (New York: Norton, 1933), p. 95.

[22] *Ibid.*, p. 84.

[23] W. Lloyd Warner and James Abegglen, *Big Business Leaders in America* (New York: Harper, 1955), Ch. 5. See also Franz Alexander, "Educative Influence of Personality Factors in the Environment," in Clyde Kluckhohn, Henry A. Murray, and David M. Schneider (eds.), *Personality in Nature, Society, and Culture* (2nd ed.; New York: Knopf, 1953), pp. 431–2.

[24] See Bronislaw Malinowski, *Sex and Repression in Savage Society* (New York: Meridian, 1955).

[25] See, for example, Abram Kardiner *et al.*, *The Psychological Frontiers of Society* (New York: Columbia University Press, 1945).

[26] Theodore Adorno *et al.*, *The Authoritarian Personality* (New York: Harper, 1950).

[27] Margaret Mead, *Growing Up in New Guinea* (New York: Morrow, 1930).

[28] See Stanton Wheeler, "The Structure of Formally Organized Socialization Settings," in Orville G. Brim, Jr., and Stanton Wheeler, *Socialization After Childhood: Two Essays* (New York: Wiley, 1966), pp. 51–116.

[29] Robert M. MacIver and Charles H. Page, *Society: An Introductory Analysis* (New York: Holt, 1949), p. 217.

[30] See John W. M. Whiting and Irvin L. Child, *Child Training and Personality: A Cross-Cultural Study* (New Haven: Yale University Press, 1953).

[31] Aristotle, *Politics,* trans. by William Ellis (New York: Dutton, 1939), p. 213.

[32] Leo Tolstoy, *War and Peace,* trans. by Louis and Aylmer Maude (New York: Simon & Schuster, 1942), p. 709.

[33] Wright Miller, *Russians as People* (New York: Dutton, 1961), pp. 88–9.

[34] See Alex Inkeles, "Personality and Social Structure," in Robert K. Merton, Leonard Broom, and Leonard S. Cottrell, Jr. (eds.), *Sociology Today* (New York: Basic Books, 1959), pp. 249–76.

[35] See Kardiner, *op. cit.,* Chs. 5–9. The report of the field research is in Cora Du Bois, *The People of Alor* (Minneapolis: University of Minnesota Press, 1944).

[36] David Riesman, with Reuel Denny and Nathan Glazer, *The Lonely Crowd* (New Haven: Yale University Press, 1950), p. 4.

[37] Adorno *et al., op. cit.*

[38] Robert K. Merton, *Mass Persuasion* (New York: Harper, 1946), p. 143.

[39] See, for example, Ely Chinoy, *Automobile Workers and the American Dream* (New York: Random House, 1955), Ch. 10.

[40] Ralph Linton, *The Study of Man* (New York: Appleton, 1936), p. 413.

[41] *Ibid.*

[42] Benedict, *op. cit.,* p. 234.

Suggestions for further reading

BRIM, ORVILLE G., JR., AND STANTON WHEELER. *Socialization After Childhood: Two Essays*. New York: Wiley, 1966.
Two essays dealing with adult socialization, the first on general problems, the second on socialization within formal organizations.

COHEN, YEHUDI. *Social Structure and Personality: A Casebook*. New York: Holt, 1961.
An excellent collection of research studies tied together by the author's theoretical analysis and interpretation.

COOLEY, CHARLES H. *Human Nature and the Social Order*. New York: Scribner, 1902.
An early discussion of the interdependence of individual and society that is still in some respects a classic.

DAVIS, KINGSLEY. *Human Society*. New York: Macmillan, 1947, Ch. 7, "Jealousy and Sexual Property: An Illustration."
A sociological analysis of a psychological response that examines the social conditions under which the expression of jealousy is expected or permitted and the social functions it performs.

DURKHEIM, ÉMILE. *Suicide*. Trans. by John A. Spaulding and George Simpson. New York: Free Press, 1951 (first published in 1897).
A classic example of sociological analysis of a phenomenon usually thought of in psychological terms. A major contribution to sociological theory.

ELKIN, FREDERICK. *The Child and Society: The Process of Socialization*. New York: Random House, 1960.
A brief analysis of the forms and agencies of socialization and of subcultural differences in patterns of socialization.

ERIKSON, ERIK H. *Childhood and Society*. New York: Norton, 1950.
Using a psychoanalytic approach, coupled with anthropological observation, the author explores in rich and suggestive fashion the relationship between culture and personality.

LINTON, RALPH. *The Cultural Background of Personality*. New York: Appleton, 1945.

An excellent introduction to the ways in which culture and social structure affect the development of personality.

PARSONS, TALCOTT. *Social Structure and Personality*. New York: Free Press, 1964.
A collection of essays on the interrelations of social structure and personality. See particularly Ch. 1, "The Superego and the Theory of Social Systems," which seeks to link together systematically the formation of personality and the functioning of the social order.

PIAGET, JEAN. *The Moral Judgment of the Child*. Trans. by Marjorie Gabain. New York: Free Press, 1948.
An intriguing study by a noted Swiss social psychologist of the process by which the child acquires moral standards. One of a number of important studies of socialization by the same author.

5
modes of sociological analysis

The sociological "why?"

The task of sociology, we have said, is to explain those aspects of human behavior encompassed in the concepts of culture and society. These concepts define the foci of sociological interest; they direct our attention to patterned and repetitive forms of acting, thinking, and feeling and to the organized relations among individuals and groups.

A great deal of sociological and anthropological investigation results in merely systematic description of the recurrent behavior and social relationships found in different societies or among different groups. Such factual reports, though obviously essential, constitute only the initial step in sociological inquiry, since the latter's ultimate aim is to explain or account for the facts.

In common discourse, explanation frequently means simply making some phenomenon more understandable; it is "simplification, paraphrase, and description," [1] and may be achieved by analogy, example, or by restatement in other words. Scientific explanation, on the other hand, consists in showing or identifying the conditions under which events take place, or their relations to other events. It seeks to answer the question: "Why?"

"Why?" is perhaps as much a weasel word as any in our entire vocabulary. The question is usually asked with some implicit expectation of the kind of answer desired, of the terms in which the answer is to be given. For example, the question, "Why do people commit suicide?" is not the same for the psychologist and the sociologist. The former wants to know why a particular individual takes his own life. The latter is asking why suicide is more frequent in some groups than in others and what conditions account for changes in the frequency with which it occurs. "Why?" states the existence of a question; it does not specify its precise character. Our immediate task, therefore, is to spell out the nature of the sociological "Why?" [2]

Within sociology itself there are as many answers to the question "Why?" as there are alternative sociological theories. Among the substantial array of sociological explanations, however, two major approaches may be distinguished, each resting upon different assumptions, asking different kinds of questions, and expecting different answers. We shall call these approaches the "functional" and the "historical." The older terms by which they have been identified are "static" and "dynamic," terms which go back to Auguste Comte, the founder of sociology as a distinctive discipline, although the latter term has now come to have a different meaning. On occasion these alternative approaches have also been described as "synchronic" and "diachronic."

In the continuing process of conceptual analysis and development, all of these terms have undergone refinement and redefinition. Like most other sociological concepts, *social function* has been considerably revised and elaborated upon since it first appeared in systematic form in Émile Durkheim's *The Rules of Sociological Method* in 1895. The term *dynamics,* which for Comte meant social change and social evolution, has now come to have a significant place in the usually ahistorical approach of functionalism, referring to the processes by which a social system is maintained. Early sociologists were greatly concerned with history and the evolution of society; after a long period during which the idea of evolution was largely ignored, it has recently reappeared in sociological discussion, albeit in a somewhat revised form.[3]

The functional approach, although sometimes defined in special ways and containing difficult and important problems yet to be resolved, has come to possess a generally understood and accepted meaning.[4] It sees a society as a more or less integrated whole. Explanation consists in showing the place of social norms, beliefs, patterns of behavior, social relationships, and values in the entire structure and in relation to one another. Functionalism's fundamental question has to do with the maintenance of social order or of a "social system."

The historical approach, though it too may view a society as a whole, is concerned chiefly with change, with the development and transformation of institutions, beliefs and values, patterns of behavior, and forms of organization. Instead of asking how a society hangs together and what keeps it going as a more or less integrated whole, it seeks to define the processes of change, the conditions under which it occurs, and the consequences of various kinds of change for the social order.

The functional and the historical are not contradictory approaches to sociological phenomena; rather they complement one another, and will in all likelihood become more and more closely linked together as our understanding of both the structure and functioning of society and the changes taking place within it is extended.

Functional analysis

Society, we have noted, is a totality made up of interrelated and interdependent parts. From one point of view it is a complex structure of groups and individuals held together in a web of social relationships. From another, it is a system of institutions related to and reacting upon one another. From either perspective, society may be thought of as a functioning whole, as an operating system. Analogies in scientific analysis can be misleading, yet it is sometimes helpful to conceive of society as an organism, or at least as possessing some organic characteristics. The different components of society should be seen in relation to the whole; apart from that whole they lose their sociological significance. They are constantly acting and reacting upon one another, adapting themselves or being adapted in various ways to changes or processes occurring in other segments of society. An essential task of sociology, therefore, is to explain the functioning of society and to explore the relations between the parts and the whole and among the parts themselves.

The concept of *function,* which has come in recent years to play an increasingly important role in performing this task, is "neither new nor confined to the social sciences." [5] It occupies a significant position in such varied disciplines as biology, psychology, physics, and architecture. In the social sciences the concept has developed in an uneven fashion, "in shreds and patches," to use Robert Merton's phrase, with now one, now another, aspect emphasized. But the presupposition upon which the concept—and the mode of analysis associated with the concept—is based, namely that phenomena must be seen "in terms of interconnection of operation rather than in terms of separate . . . units" [6] has remained unchanged and unchallenged.

The idea contained in the pioneer formulation of Émile Durkheim, of course, was not new. It can be found frequently in the work of Karl Marx and of Herbert Spencer, the nineteenth-century evolutionary thinker against whose ideas Durkheim was contending. As an organism or aggregate (individual or social) becomes more complex, Spencer asserted, "that combination of actions which constitutes the life of the whole makes possible the component actions which constitute the lives of the parts." [7] Durkheim's contribution lay in his clear differentiation of the analysis of social functions from the analysis of the development and evolution of social forms. "When . . . the explanation of a social phenomenon is undertaken," he wrote, "we must seek separately the efficient cause which produces it and the function it fulfills." [8]

The concept of function refers to the "observable objective consequences" of social phenomena as they relate to social structure, institutional systems, and culturally patterned sentiments, values, and beliefs. The phenomena with which sociology is concerned are those encompassed by the concepts thus far examined: cultural patterns, institutions, values, roles, social relationships—as well as other more precisely defined and conceptualized social phenomena. Any regularity, that is, any patterned or repetitive behavior, interaction, or emotional response, can therefore be subjected to functional analysis.

The explanatory significance of "function" can be simply stated. If we seek to account for some social fact in functional terms we try to identify its relations to other elements in society, conceived of as an ongoing system of interdependent parts in which the item studied has positive results, that is, it makes possible other activities or sustains other patterned, repetitive social or cultural forms. In effect, we ask: What are the consequences of the item studied for other elements of the structure, or for the structure as a whole?

Such analysis may be carried on at different levels. On the most general level one may consider the contribution of any social or cultural item to the survival, persistence, integration, or stability of a society as a whole. The functions of the family in any society include, at least, bringing new members into the society, providing for their physical maintenance, transmitting to them a large part of the culture which they need to know (the process of "socialization"), and giving them their initial position, or status, in the social structure. This general level of functional analysis has sometimes been stretched to include the satisfaction of those needs of individuals—food, shelter, sexual gratification, and emotional response—without which human life could not persist. The warrant for this extension of the concept of function to physiological and psychological categories lies in the fact that in some measure all societies focus their social and cultural organization upon the satisfaction of these needs. The family, for example, almost always provides an approved channel (though not necessarily the only appropriate one) for satisfying sexual desires, as well as offering the possibility of other significant emotional experience.

Analysis of the functions of institutions and social structures for society as a whole has often been coupled with efforts to identify and delineate the *functional requisites* that must be met if a society—any society—is to persist and survive.[9] Sociologists have defined these requisites in various ways, although they tend to agree that every society must provide for biological reproduction and survival, for socializing new members and motivating them to carry out

socially necessary roles, and for maintaining some degree
of social order. In addition to these minimum requirements, others have been suggested about which there is
little agreement. The importance of the definition of functional requisites (a theoretical task not yet adequately performed) lies in part in the attempt to account for the
presence of universal culture patterns and social structures
—family, religion, political controls, and so on—by relating
them to the fundamental requirements for sustained group
life.

The attempt to explain specific cultural and social
phenomena on the basis of the functional requisites they
satisfy often rests upon an implicit definition of the limits
or boundaries of a particular society. Such a definition is
clearly necessary in order to examine the functions of institutions and social structures for the total social order.
But various criteria can be used in order to establish limits
of an inclusive social system. In a "primitive" tribe the
limits are likely to be fairly clear-cut, set by shared cultural
patterns and a system of social relationships largely or totally
confined within the group. The social unit is adequately set
off by the shared loyalties to a total social code. In modern
societies, however, the limits are likely to be defined in most
cases by political organization and boundaries. That this
can be theoretically justified stems from two facts: Power
and politics play a particularly important role in the life
of modern societies, and political boundaries usually coincide with significant cultural divisions. Yet in some instances,
in parts of Europe and the Near East, for example, ethnic
and political boundaries are not congruent. Thus in Belgium the division between Flemish and Walloons has been
for many years a constant source of friction and antagonism,
which appear now to be increasing. In Iraq a dissident
Kurdish minority resists the central authority, and in
Morocco efforts to create a modern state and society have
run into difficulties because of a sizable Berber minority

in an otherwise largely Arab population. Failure to recognize these facts may lead to inaccurate or misleading conclusions about the total societies in which these divisions exist.

Functional analysis therefore often focuses upon "subsystems," or subgroups, or subcultures, within the larger whole—upon the economy, or polity (the institutions and collectivities relevant to the structure of power), for example, or upon the kinship system, the value system, or some complex organizational structure. It is often fruitful to look upon each of these components or aspects of a total social order from a functional point of view, inquiring into its dynamics and how it is sustained, as well as examining its relationships to other subsystems or to the society as a whole.

Concern with functional requisites may lead—indeed in some cases has led—to assumptions about the inevitability of specific institutions and forms of organization. These assumptions derive from the neglect of *functional alternatives,* that is, those institutions or social structures which can perform the same or similar functions. In addition, if attention is concentrated chiefly on the ways in which a specific rule or belief or structure serves the society as a whole, the full range of its consequences may remain unexamined. Concepts and questions, we pointed out earlier, focus attention upon some phenomena and consequently tend to exclude other matters from observation; they are ways of not-seeing as well as of seeing. By focusing attention upon the contributions of religion to social stability, for example, many writers have ignored alternative ways of maintaining stability and the frequently divisive and disruptive effects of religion as well.[10] Similarly, a general analysis of government as an institutional system, the principal functions of which are to maintain social order by resolving disputes and to enforce conformity to important social norms, may result in the neglect of the problem

of what kind of order: authoritarian or democratic, hierarchical or equalitarian, traditional or rational.

The analysis of the functions of any feature of a society
must include not only its contribution to the total social
order but also its consequences for particular groups and
institutions within the society. The careful scheduling of
railroad operations, to cite a familiar illustration, obviously
contributes to the efficient performance of essential social
tasks in an industrial society. But the functional significance
of the careful timing and ordering of operations must also
be seen in relation to diverse groups and a variety of institutionalized activities. For some industries reliable train
schedules are necessary in order to maintain the continuous
flow of production; if, for example, a large nylon plant does
not receive regular shipments of the chemical ingredients it
needs, the whole manufacturing process would be inter-
rupted. For the stockholder, the more efficient the performance of the railroad, the higher may be his return. For the
commuter, adherence to railroad timetables makes possible
a regular and predictable pattern of daily behavior: He
can shower, shave, drink his morning coffee, and kiss his
wife good-by secure in the knowledge that if he arrives at
the station as late as 8:29½ A.M. he will still be able to beat
the boss to the office. For small-town cab drivers, the sched-
uled arrival of trains passing through may dictate a regular
feature of their daily routine and provide a source of fares.
For the railroad employee, the rigorous demands of train
schedules influence his working hours and his whole pattern
of life. He becomes enormously sensitive to time and is likely
to demand punctuality in all contexts. Since he must adapt
himself to timetable requirements, he may not be able to
follow the normal day-by-day routines of other people; he
will frequently have to spend nights as well as days away
from home and may have to work on Saturdays, Sundays,
and holidays when others are enjoying time off from their

labors. These facts may in turn affect his family life and participation in community affairs.[11]

Manifest and latent functions

As a close examination of this illustration will indicate, some of the functions of railroad schedules are intended and desired while others are either unintended or unknown to the persons directly involved. It is essential, therefore, in examining the functions of social and cultural forms to distinguish between the purposes or goals they are supposed to achieve and the actual consequences which flow from them. The effects of regular train schedules on railroad employees and small-town taxi-drivers are clearly unanticipated consequences of rules made in order to achieve other objectives. Or, to take another illustration, we buy clothing to protect us from the elements, to satisfy our own standards of taste, to please or impress our family, friends, and perhaps, our neighbors. Whatever our aims, however, our clothing in fact identifies and contributes to our status, or standing, in the community, as do many of the activities we normally carry on for a wide variety of reasons.

Purpose and result frequently do not completely coincide: What is intended is often not achieved. There is no evidence, for example, that rain dances by the Zuñi bring rain, or that many of the rites and ritual incantations of healers in primitive societies cure disease, despite the beliefs and intentions of dancers and watchers, of healers and their patients. That this is so, however, does not mean that such patterned activities have no important social functions.

A distinction must therefore be drawn between *manifest* and *latent* functions. Manifest functions are those consequences for society or any of its subsystems or segments that are "intended and recognized by participants in the system." Latent functions are those consequences that are "neither intended nor recognized." [12]

The line between these two types of functions is neither fixed nor always easy to draw. Latent consequences may at times become quite apparent. Several years ago women in a university dormitory were offered the total elimination of curfew restrictions. To the surprise of the Dean, they refused. They had suddenly realized the advantages inherent in a rule that gave them a legitimate excuse for an early good night to an unsuccessful date.

The functions of particular institutions or values may be manifest to some persons and not to others. Edward Gibbon, for example, in describing the various religions prevalent in ancient Rome observed that they "were all considered by the people as equally true; by the philosopher, as equally false; and by the magistrate, as equally useful." [13] While most American Catholics at the turn of the century probably did not conceive of their religion as an instrument for minimizing social or political discontent, President Taft described it as "one of the bulwarks against socialism and anarchy in this country." [14] Two leading businessmen, "a Nordic Protestant, James J. Hill, and a Semitic skeptic, Max Pam, gave generous sums to Catholic institutions for the avowed purpose of helping to spread discipline over the restive working classes of the land." [15] Similarly, as Liston Pope reported in his study of a North Carolina mill town in the 1930s, some Baptist and Methodist manufacturers helped support dissident Protestant sects because they provided a noneconomic and nonpolitical outlet for the frustrations generated by low wages and poor working conditions,[16] a function that sect members could hardly be aware of.

Despite the occasional inability to identify specific functions as either manifest or latent, formulating the distinction leads us consciously to explore in every case the unnoticed consequences of institutions, beliefs, and forms of organization. As Merton has pointed out, by examining the latent functions of "seemingly irrational social patterns"—magic and superstition, for example—it is possible to explain their place and persistence in the social scheme of things. Although a rain dance is not likely to produce rain, it may well relieve anxiety and bring more closely together the members of the society, and reinforce—or raise—the social status of some of the participants as well. These more or less latent functions may provide a reasonably adequate explanation for the persistence of such ritual, despite its failure to achieve its manifest aims.

Similarly, the persistence of illicit patterns of action such as political corruption or gambling can also be explained in considerable measure by reference to the latent functions they serve in American society. Political corruption, as it develops in political machines, for example, often "humanizes" and "personalizes" the operation of government. In addition to its less applauded consequences, such as increasing the cost of government and favoring private interests at the expense of the public interest, it offers an avenue of social mobility to some persons, and provides a source of income not only for party hacks but also for businessmen and racketeers who can do business with the machine.[17] Gambling, when it is not institutionally sanctioned, often thrives among persons whose lives are otherwise closely ordered; it provides them with variety and excitement usually unavailable to them. Among those with few opportunities for wealth or even occasional affluence, gambling, in the numbers racket, for example, offers a chance for gain otherwise not possible for them.

The social consequences of institutional patterns and social structures, as even cursory examination discloses—and as our illustrations suggest—are not always advantageous for the whole society or for some of its component parts. Any single pattern may have both negative and positive results. The American belief that anyone who has "what it takes" can "get ahead in the world," for example, may stimulate ambition (a quality valued by Americans) and reinforce loyalties to American institutions (which provide the opportunities ostensibly open to everyone), but it may also encourage vain hopes and lead to frustration, guilt, and self-blame among those who fail to succeed, whether because of personal limitations or social obstacles. Informal limitation of output among factory workers, a fact frequently documented in industrial studies, may perform significant functions for the workers: protection against the "speed-up" and against layoffs because of fulfilled contracts, as well as direct satisfactions simply from participation in the group. But workers' restriction of output obviously limits the efficiency of industrial operations. The use of terror by a totalitarian regime helps it to maintain power but clearly creates difficulties for many of its citizens—and may inhibit the growth of spontaneous social groups outside the "official" bureaucratically organized structure.

In order to focus attention systematically upon the negative consequences of social patterns, as well as the positive, the concept of *dysfunction* is often employed to refer to those consequences that tend to diminish the integration or stability of a society or any of its component parts and to lessen the possibility of survival and persistence.

To summarize, functional analysis, we may then say, consists of the exploration of the full range of social and cultural consequences, both manifest and latent, positive and negative (which may be either manifest or latent), of any institutional pattern or social structure. Marion Levy has suggested that because the term *function* encompasses all of these possibilities, one should distinguish between *eufunction* (the positive contribution to the success or stability of a structure) and *dysfunction* (the negative consequences).[18] As the meaning is usually clear from the context, these neologisms are not always necessary, although the distinction they imply should be kept clearly in mind.

In order to discover the functions—and dysfunctions—of any social pattern it is necessary to locate it in the specific social and cultural context in which it occurs. Frequently the social structure and culture generate the very problems or needs to whose resolution or satisfaction the item contributes. Without an understanding of the nature and sources of economic or political discontent, for example, it would be difficult to assay the way in which religion meets that discontent. Further, the same pattern can serve different functions in different contexts. Emphasis upon individual advancement in a rapidly expanding society encourages innovation and creativity; in a relatively stable society with limited opportunities it may lead only to considerable frustration and illegal experiments—or to revolutionary change.

Functional analysis: three cases

We may illustrate more fully the nature of functional analysis with three cases drawn from very different social contexts.

"Rituals of Rebellion" Among Zulu Women

In his analysis of South African rituals, Max Gluckman describes agricultural rites performed by women at the time when planting is begun each year.

> The young unmarried girls donned men's garments and carried shields and assagais [spears]. They drove the cattle out to pasture and milked them, though cattle were normally taboo to females. Meanwhile their mothers planned a garden for the goddess [Nomkubulwana] far out in the veld, and poured a libation of beer to her. Thereafter this garden was neglected. At various stages of the ceremonies women and girls went naked, and sang lewd songs. Men and boys hid

inside the huts, and might not go near the women. If they did, the women and girls could attack them.[19]

These rituals were felt to be of positive value, and to be important in securing a good crop.

The functions of these rituals, in which women "committed public obscenities and acted as if they were men," can be understood only in relation to the position of women in Zulu society.

> . . . a woman was in law—in law, not always in practice—subject to the control of some man—either her father or brother, or after marriage her husband. The prime effect of this subordination was to give these men control over the woman's capacities as wife and as child-bearer. In exchange for transferring to the husband a woman's capacity as a wife, including her work in the gardens, and her capacity as a bearer of children, the husband handed over to her male relatives cattle which were taboo to her—she could not touch them or go into their corral. . . .
>
> . . . the approach of marriage was a period of great distress for Zulu girls: they were subject to frequent attacks of hysteria which were ascribed to the love-magic of their suitors. Marriage itself was a difficult relation, requiring adjustment to a strange family where the girl was hedged with many taboos. She had to avoid important parts of her husband's home village and even parts of her own hut. She had to alter her language so as not to use any word containing the root of her husband's name or the names of her senior male relatives-in-law. Her stressed function was to be a dutiful, hard-working, faithful, and decorous wife, bearing children for her husband, and caring for those children. Only when they grew up could she become independent, as the mother of grown sons.[20]

The difficulties in the woman's position were further complicated by the peculiarities of the Zulu system for reckoning descent and determining inheritance.

The annual rituals, therefore, provided an opportunity to engage in normally prohibited behavior. "Allowing [the women] to herd the cattle would be a reward and a release, especially while they were also allowed to go naked and sing lewd songs and attack wandering men. This statement, that performing these normally tabooed actions is a reward and release, seems to be justified by the descriptions we have. But part of its interpretation involves psychological analysis for which there is [as yet] no evidence." [21] Although there has been no systematic research into the psychological aspects of this interpretation, there does appear to be evidence, largely clinical in character, that an emotional catharsis does enable people to continue to function effectively in situations in which there are built-in sources of tension.

In addition to these social-psychological functions, "the lifting of the normal taboos and restraints obviously serves to emphasize [conventional rules] . . . this particular ritual, by allowing people to behave in normally prohibited ways, gave expression, in a reversed form, to the normal rightness of a particular kind of social order." [22] The functions of these rituals, then, included at least the resolution of tensions created by the social structure, and the reinforcement of existing norms and relationships; in generating these results the rituals help to sustain the whole system of family roles and relationships, which in this case meant virtually the entire fabric of the society.

The Tolkach in Soviet Society

In 1959, *Izvestia,* the official government newspaper in the Soviet Union, published a lengthy article excoriating the *tolkachi* (literally "pushers"), who worked as agents for plant managers, locating scarce materials they needed and making arrangements for their delivery. Many of the activities of the *tolkachi* resembled those of expediters in American industry, whose task is to assure the delivery of needed

supplies. But in order to secure the raw materials or components that were required by his client, the *tolkach* often
had to persuade officials to ignore the plans they were supposed to be following, either through persuasion, personal
influence, or *sub rosa* gifts and exchanges. According to
Izvestia, one factory in the Urals had sent out 2,762 *tolkachi*
in an eleven-month period, a steel mill had dispatched
2,813 and one factory in the Gorki district had been host to
approximately 3,000 *tolkachi* within an eight-month span.[23]

In an economy in which production is carefully planned,
with each plant required to achieve a given output and with
careful provision for deliveries of required supplies, the
widespread phenomenon of the *tolkach,* who operated on the
thin edge of legality, would seem to be something of an
anomaly. Yet he survived despite the official criticism, for
he served important functions. No over-all plan can foresee
all the problems that might interfere with the operations
of a complex economy, in which failure to achieve a set
goal in one plant may precipitate a sequence of failures in
other plants when needed supplies are not forthcoming. As
the Soviet Union has sought to achieve a continued high
rate of industrialization and economic growth, building
new plants, training a labor force, introducing new techniques, some such failures have been perhaps inevitable.
Yet little allowance is made for the many exigencies that
can develop, and plant managers are held responsible for
the quotas they have been assigned. In these circumstances,
it would hardly be surprising if plant managers had recourse
to the quasi-legal *tolkach* who might be able to secure the
necessary supplies.

The consequences of the frequently criticized activities
of the *tolkach* could be both functional and dysfunctional
for the economy as a whole. Barrington Moore sums up
these consequences as follows:

> By interfering with the intricate system of priorities he per-
> forms a definite disservice to the regime. On the other hand,

by scaring up supplies that may be useless where they are, but are badly needed by his employer, he performs a definite service for the economy. Possibly his positive contributions outweigh his disadvantages in the eyes of the authorities, who therefore continue to tolerate his existence.[24]

The steadily increasing productivity of the Soviet economy, which is probably eliminating chronic shortages of some materials, and the various changes that have been made in the organization and administration of the economy since 1959, however, may have diminished the need for the free-wheeling *tolkach*. In any event, there has been little mention of the *tolkach* in recent years in either the Soviet press or the writings of students of the Soviet Union.

American "Baby Manuals"

A Manual of Child Care, by Benjamin Spock, was first published in 1946 and then reprinted in a paperback edition which went through 58 printings. A revised paperback edition subsequently went through 150 printings by 1965, and according to its publishers the book had sold over 16 million copies since its first appearance. The Children's Bureau published *Infant Care,* a somewhat briefer guide book, in 1914, and has since revised it ten times, more recently in 1963. An estimated 40 million copies have been distributed. These are only the most popular and widely used of a large array of baby-care manuals that provide American mothers (and fathers) with suggestions and directions for looking after children and for dealing with the many problems they face: health, feeding, toilet-training, sex education, discipline, and so on.

Why this extraordinary and by now steady and familiar pattern of using published child-care manuals? One obvious explanation would be the growth of scientific knowledge in both medicine and psychology in recent decades and the mounting public respect for science. But this explanation in itself is incomplete, for it overlooks those changes in family structure that lead people to seek such knowledge. Why do so many parents not rely, as their parents did before them, upon time-tested and traditional methods of child care handed down from mother to daughter, with such modifications as creep into traditional routines from time to time? The answer lies in large measure in the structure of the contemporary American family.

The modern American household is typically limited to parents and their children; resident in-laws are, on the whole, strongly disapproved of. Moreover, in our highly mobile society, many of these "nuclear" or "elementary" families, as they are called, are likely to live some distance from their respective parents, and from uncles, aunts, and cousins. In addition, the typical family is relatively small and the intervals between children short. Many girls, consequently, have little opportunity to witness or learn traditional methods of caring for small children. The shifting roles of women now include, in addition to childbearing and child care, other activities looked on as necessary, proper, and desirable; there are, therefore, no strong incentives and only limited opportunity in many cases to acquire in advance the skills of motherhood. As a result the young mother is likely to have little practical knowledge when her own children arrive, and parents or relatives who might be helpful are not easily accessible. She must, therefore, secure information, advice, and aid from other sources. In a society that places so much stress upon science, suggestions from appropriately qualified professionals are likely to carry heavy weight. The function of these baby-care manuals, then, is to fill the gap in knowledge left by the particular structure of the modern-day family. They provide methods for dealing with recurrent problems for which there are few traditional solutions available and hardly any other sources of aid.

The use of such child-care literature, however, is more frequent in the middle class than in the working class. In a recent study, Zena Blau found that 77 per cent of a sample of white middle-class mothers had read Dr. Spock's book, compared with only 48 per cent among working-class mothers.[25] This difference reflects class differences in family structure, values, and knowledge. Middle-class families have typically been smaller (though this difference has been diminishing). More significantly, they are better educated (91 per cent of the middle-class women had graduated from high school or attended college, compared with only 45 per cent of the working-class women) and more approving of the findings of modern medical and psychological science. They are also more likely to see child-rearing as "problematic" and therefore to seek out expert aid and advice than are working-class parents, who are inclined to be quite satisfied with traditional methods of child care.[26]

Social change and the "historical" approach

Functional analysis in general and each of the specific concepts we have thus far introduced presume a considerable degree of stability and constancy in human behavior. One cannot examine a social role without assuming that the norms governing behavior persist over a period of time. An assertion that a particular belief contributes to the persistence of some institutional system obviously implies that both belief and institutions have some measure of continuity. Yet it is also readily apparent that though many things seem to remain the same, other aspects of society are continually changing. In a world so frequently described as revolutionary, this point hardly needs emphasis. Sociological analysis, therefore, must account not only for stability and continuity, but also for the transformation of society and culture and for the introduction of new ideas, new habits, new relationships, new forms of organization.

The problems of change, of course, are not new to

sociology, which has deep roots in eighteenth- and nineteenth-century philosophies of history. Beginning with
Comte and his predecessors—for example, Henri de Saint
Simon—and continuing through the rest of the nineteenth
century and into the twentieth, most sociologists devoted
their attention chiefly to problems of social change. The
central questions for Comte, Herbert Spencer, and Lester
F. Ward concerned the processes and the sequences through
which society had evolved. These evolutionary theories made
frequent assumptions about the inevitability of progress,
the superiority of modern society, and the proper place of
sociological knowledge itself. They began with origins:
How did the family first come into being? Or religion? Or
the state? Having established theories of origins, they then
sought to trace the successive stages through which institutions had developed. Often they applied the concepts and
theories of biological evolution: natural selection, survival
of the fittest, adaptation.

These problems are of comparatively little interest to
contemporary scholars. As Robert M. MacIver and Charles
H. Page have observed: "The seed of society is in the beginnings of life, and if there were . . . beginnings [of society]
in any absolute sense we know nothing of them." [27] The
theory of unilineal social evolution, which held that each
society passes through the same stages of development, has
been entirely abandoned. Evolution, as a guiding principle,
no longer has much currency among sociologists or anthropologists, except for a few scholars who continue to use the
concept, albeit in a refined and sophisticated form. One of
these contemporary scholars, Julian Steward, sums up his
version of evolutionary theory as follows: "The methodology
of evolution . . . postulates that genuine parallels of form
and function develop in historically independent sequences
or cultural traditions. Second, it explains these parallels by
the independent operation of identical causality in each
case." [28] By examining the emergence of roughly similar

social forms in different societies it might then be possible
to arrive at valid conclusions concerning the development
of institutional systems and social structures. This type of
formulation does not differ very much from prevailing
theoretical views except in its assumption that it may
eventually be possible to develop a general theory of evolution applicable to all social groups.

The general failure of evolutionary theory—and its re-
jection—stemmed from two related weaknesses. The mechanical application of ideas derived from one field of
inquiry to another (a tactic utilized by some students of
man and society in order to create a seemingly scientific
discipline) almost inevitably distorted the facts by coercing
them into preconceived schemes. More significantly, perhaps, evolutionary theorists could not reach agreement on
the criteria that distinguished the more evolved from the
less evolved, the more complex from the less complex,
particularly in the light of new knowledge concerning non-
Western societies and cultures. A seemingly simple society
among the Australian aborigines, for example, possessing a
crude technology and subsisting on hunting and food gather-
ing, was found to have an extremely complex kinship system
and elaborate ceremonials.[29]

The development of functional theory was in part a
reaction to the inadequacies of evolutionary thought and an
effort to explore the interrelations of social institutions and
social structures. There now appears to be a swing back
toward a renewed interest in evolution, though within the
context of the knowledge we now possess of the structure
and functioning of society. Talcott Parsons, for example,
perhaps the leading sociological "functionalist," in a paper
which he defined as a "contribution to the revival and examination of evolutionary thinking in sociology," has sought
to identify, in a very general fashion, a sequence of "evolutionary universals," each of which constitutes a necessary
prerequisite for the development of new and more complex

levels of social organization.[30] In a much less abstract formulation, Wilbert Moore has asserted that "there has been a
long-term increase in man's ability to adapt to and control
his environment." There are several "long-term trends"
which, he argues, are "consistent" with this assertion: the
increase in the size of human populations, the "additive or
accumulative character of objective knowledge and rational
technique," the accelerating rate at which knowledge can
be acquired and stored, and the incorporation of all men
into a "*single*" system," despite persisting conflicts and differences among human groups.[31]

These new evolutionary formulations, however, though
raising important long-run questions, are so general that
they still have only limited value in accounting for the
specific complex changes that take place in institutions,
values, beliefs, social structures, and patterns of social behavior. Yet an historical approach must seek to explain
these changes. While the functional approach focuses upon
the mechanisms by which an existing social order is
maintained, the historical directs attention to the forces
and processes that contribute to the flux and variation of
social life.

The contrast between the functional and historical approaches, however, is sometimes mistakenly described as a
distinction between the static and the dynamic. Both approaches must deal with social processes taking place over a
period of time even though they order and interpret their
observations differently. To see a society as a functioning
whole is not to see it as unmoving or standing still; if we
may borrow an image from biology, the vital processes of
social life, the complex reciprocal adjustments and responses
of individuals, organizations, and institutions to one another, continue wherever men live together in society.
Within any social order there are processes of varying
degrees of complexity, more or less regular sequences of
events in which men conform to established norms and fit

into some existing social structures. Functional analysis deals with such processes within a relatively stable structure in which the participants may change and individuals may move from one role or status to another. The historical approach is concerned with the processes by which the structure itself is changed.

Before one can deal with problems of social change, it has been argued, one must first understand the functional dynamics of society. There seems to be little warrant for this asserted priority; insofar as inquiry begins with facts to be explained one can as readily begin with the facts of change as with the facts of stability. But wherever one begins, one must eventually deal with both sets of facts, to maintain, as it were, a double focus. Both views, the historical and functional, presuppose that society is a whole or system made up of interrelated and interdependent parts.

Many theories of social change have emphasized one factor—or one part in the total complex—while underestimating or neglecting others: Karl Marx's economic determinism, Thorstein Veblen's technological determinism, theories that assign crucial importance to ideology or religion or to geography and climate. These monistic interpretations attribute an independent and dynamic character to a single factor; as it is transformed other elements in the society are affected and eventually change their form or function. These theories have frequently called attention, when first put forward, to previously ignored or underestimated historical forces, but they all inevitably oversimplify the causes and processes of change.

So interconnected are the various elements of society that no one set of institutions or social structures, no matter how important it may be, can be said to be unaffected by others—self-caused, so to speak. (The gross "factors" in these theories—Marx's "economic base," Veblen's technology, for example—are so conceived, in any case, that in effect they include several readily distinguished variables.) The course of economic development can be and frequently is markedly influenced by political or religious institutions. Ideas and beliefs do not exist in an ivory tower free from the influence of the market place or the political arena. The pursuit of power and authority is often directed to ends defined by economic or religious values, which can in turn affect the very nature of political organization. What is important in one era may be more or less important in another: Strictly economic factors probably played a much greater role in the nineteenth century than they do in the mid-twentieth. As C. Wright Mills commented: "We do not know any universal principles of historical change; the mechanisms of change we do know vary with the social structure we are examining. For historical change *is* change of social structures, of the relations among their component parts. Just as there is a variety of social structures, there is a variety of principles of historical change." [32]

In the absence of any over-all theory of social change, we shall suggest only some general perspectives to guide our discussion. Sources of change may be exogenous, that is, come from outside the society, or endogenous, that is, from within. The latter can be either institutionally sanctioned types of innovation or the tensions, strains, and conflicts generated within the society itself.

Diffusion

As the world has become more closely knit together, with greater frequency of contact among members of different societies and an increased flow of information and ideas from one to another, the diffusion of cultural forms has increased. Americans dance the tango, Frenchmen drink Coca-Cola, and the Japanese play baseball.

The concept of *diffusion*, the spread of cultural traits

from one society to another (or from one place or group to another within the same society), was first proposed as an alternative to the evolutionary explanation for the appearance of similar characteristics in different societies. That such transfer has always been frequent is indisputable, despite the strongly nationalistic biases which lead citizens of some countries, including our own, to ignore the extent of their cultural indebtedness to others. As Ralph Linton has pointed out in a much-quoted passage:

Our solid American citizen awakens in a bed built on a pattern which originated in the Near East but which was modified in Northern Europe before it was transmitted to America. He throws back covers made from cotton, domesticated in India, or linen, domesticated in the Near East, . . . or silk, the use of which was discovered in China. All of these materials have been spun and woven by processes invented in the Near East. He slips into his moccasins, invented by the Indians of the Eastern woodlands, and goes to the bathroom, whose fixtures are a mixture of European and American inventions, both of recent date. He takes off his pajamas, a garment invented in India, and washes with soap invented by the ancient Gauls. He then shaves, a masochistic rite which seems to have been derived from either Sumer or ancient Egypt.

Returning to the bedroom, he removes his clothes from a chair of southern European type and proceeds to dress. He puts on garments whose form originally derived from the skin clothing of the nomads of the Asiatic steppes, puts on shoes made from skins tanned by a process invented in ancient Egypt and cut to a pattern derived from the classical civilizations of the Mediterranean, and ties around his neck a strip of bright-colored cloth which is a vestigial survival of the shoulder shawls worn by the seventeenth-century Croatians. Before going out for breakfast he glances through the window, made of glass invented in Egypt, and if it is raining puts on overshoes made of rubber discovered by the Central American Indians and takes an umbrella, invented in south-eastern Asia. Upon his head he puts a hat made of felt, a material invented in the Asiatic steppes.

On his way to breakfast he stops to buy a paper, paying for it with coins, an ancient Lydian invention. At the restaurant a whole new series of borrowed elements confronts him. His plate is made of a form of pottery invented in China. His knife is of steel, an alloy first made in southern India, his fork a medieval Italian invention, and his spoon a derivative of a Roman original. He begins breakfast with an orange, from the eastern Mediterranean, a cantaloupe from Persia, or perhaps a piece of African watermelon. With this he has coffee, an Abyssinian plant, with cream and sugar. Both the domestication of cows and the idea of milking them originated in the Near East, while sugar was first made in India. After his fruit and first coffee he goes on to waffles, cakes made by a Scandinavian technique from wheat domesticated in Asia Minor. Over these he pours maple syrup, invented by the Indians of the Eastern woodlands. As a side dish he may have the egg of a species of bird domesticated in Indo-China, or thin strips of the flesh of an animal domesticated in Eastern Asia which have been salted and smoked by a process developed in northern Europe.

When our friend has finished eating he settles back to smoke, an American Indian habit, consuming a plant domesticated in Brazil in either a pipe, derived from the Indians of Virginia, or a cigarette, derived from Mexico. If he is hardy enough he may even attempt a cigar, transmitted to us from the Antilles by way of Spain. While smoking he reads the news of the day, imprinted in characters invented by the ancient Semites upon a material invented in China by a process invented in Germany. As he absorbs the accounts of foreign troubles he will, if he is a good conservative citizen, thank a Hebrew deity in an Indo-European language that he is 100 per cent American.[33]

Diffusion is a selective process. As much or more may be rejected as is accepted by a society which comes in contact with new and different social and cultural patterns. Alien ideas and practices that run counter to well-established beliefs and values are rejected, and those imported cultural traits that are adopted must "fit" in some fashion into the culture, or answer some felt need derived from existing circumstances. The Japanese, for example, adopted much of Western technology, which enabled them to achieve desired goals, without simultaneously taking over Western political beliefs, institutions, art forms, philosophy, or eating habits. Only recently, as traditional verities have been challenged in the years after the Japanese defeat in World War II, have Japanese youth adopted many Western habits, attitudes, and leisure interests.

Not all exogenous change, of course, occurs gradually as new ideas are introduced through the various media of communication or through commercial, cultural, or political exchanges among members of different societies. History records many conquests in which one group of nations has forcibly imposed its power and might upon others, though even conquerors have usually had to take into account the culture and social organization of the conquered to avoid endless resistance and difficulty. In their colonial endeavors the British often exploited indigenous political arrangements, using local chiefs or rulers for their own administrative purposes. Many parts of the world even now have just emerged from colonial domination, though not without having experienced significant changes in their culture and social structure. Some of the former French colonies in Africa, for example, have adopted French parliamentary forms and carry on their debates in French, punctuated on occasion with references to classical French literature.

As nations have been incorporated into an international system of power and elaborate networks of trade and commerce, they have found it difficult to escape from the play of international political and economic forces. Even the most powerful now feel the impact of events that take place outside their boundaries.

Equilibrium and change

Yet many of the changes that occur within a society stem
from internal sources, from the normal workings of its
own institutions. In seeking out these endogenous sources
of change, it is sometimes useful to conceive of society as a
system whose equilibrium is constantly being disturbed
and in some degree re-established. By equilibrium is meant
a state of affairs in which institutions, values, and social
structures are functionally interrelated to form a more or
less integrated whole. Religious institutions sustain the
existing forms of political authority and family relationships; educational institutions inculcate accepted moral
standards and train individuals to undertake the adult roles
they are to perform; beliefs concerning the nature of human
life are fairly consistent with existing patterns of social
relationships; individuals are able to achieve the goals which
are sanctioned by the culture as important; and so on.

In a comparatively well-integrated traditional society,
the influence of external forces, peaceful or warlike, is apt
to be the major, though not the exclusive, source of change.
Within such a society, innovation is likely to be looked at
askance, and invention is infrequent, although it occasionally occurs.

Since no society is absolutely static or ever fully integrated, this equilibrium should be conceived of as dynamic
or moving and always as only partial. As changes occur and
their repercussions are felt, adjustments are made that tend
to restore the equilibrium of the system. (If appropriate
adjustments are not made, the system, of course, may fall
apart.) Within the social system of the factory, for example,
introduction of new procedures or new machines frequently
disturbs established routines and breaks up informal social
groupings among workers, requiring sometimes complex and
often difficult readjustments.

There is nothing immediate or automatic about these readjustments. They may be long delayed or long avoided, leading in some instances to pressures that explode in violent revolution or drastic, though less violent, change, followed by a new integration differing in many significant respects from the old. Thus workers who are disturbed by abrupt changes or by unresolved grievances may organize, strike, and force substantial revisions of the structure of labor-management relations.

The focus upon equilibrium or integration should not lead to a disregard of conflict or to the assumption that it merely reflects lack of integration or consensus within society. In the more extreme forms of conflict, civil war or race riots, for example, the consensus upon which society rests is challenged or destroyed. In its less violent forms, however, conflict represents a mechanism for resolving differences, thus contributing to the stability of the social order. Conflict may be an institutionalized feature of social structure: strikes or political opposition, for example; it may be tolerated as in the case of religious contentions; or it may be an inevitable consequence of the structure of society, particularly when there are many groups each seeking to realize its own ends. It has been suggested recently that a "conflict model" of society would be more fruitful than an equilibrium model;[34] certainly, as Lewis Coser has demonstrated in some detail, conflict has been ignored or underestimated in much recent sociological work.[35] But it is doubtful that there is as yet an adequate formulation of a model that can offer greater theoretical advantages than an appropriately qualified approach to society as a more or less integrated system.

In the discussion of equilibrium, as in other sociological analysis, there is sometimes a tendency to reify the concept of society, to speak of it as a "boundary-maintaining system" continually attempting to maintain its equilibrium, and of its responses to irritations or strains. Such usages normally mean that groups of persons respond in patterned ways to difficulties they face in their social lives in order to protect their established way of life or to provide for the basic necessities of collective life. To slip from this appropriate sociological shorthand into the assumption that it is the concept that acts, thinks, feels, responds, is so easy that it is important to renew the injunction against reifying what are otherwise necessary or useful abstractions.

In most modern societies, some kinds of invention and innovation, which inevitably disrupt the equilibrium of the system, are not only welcomed, but are also stimulated and encouraged. Innovation in some fields represents conformity with significant social values. Thus American society is usually receptive to new gadgets, tools, and implements (though some technical and mechanical innovations meet resistance for economic and other reasons). Efficiency and invention in industry are constantly stimulated by economic pressure. Technological innovation is encouraged in many ways: through the patent system, suggestion schemes in factories, and through a cultural emphasis upon such values and beliefs as those embodied in the traditional saying, "If a man can make a better mouse trap the world will make a beaten path to his door." The scientific progress upon which technology increasingly has come to rest is fostered through research laboratories and scientific institutes. Few other fields in the United States are equal to technology and science in their encouragement of new ideas, new devices, new routines, although in such varied segments of social life as leisure and business procedure there is a wide range of permissiveness and tolerance, as well as actual encouragement, for new techniques.

Because of the interdependence of the elements of society, change at any one point is likely to precipitate changes elsewhere. (This proposition, it should be noted, occupies a key place in the relations between functional and historical analysis.) Science and technology are therefore in effect built-in disturbers of the peace. The innovations they create are usually accepted as desirable without reference to all of their possible consequences, some of which therefore come unheralded, unpredicted, and, frequently, from the point of view of many groups, unwanted. For example, the automobile, when it first appeared, was adopted chiefly by a few members of the leisure class as a new means of recreation and display. When its practical value became apparent and its cost was reduced, largely as a result of rapid technological progress, it quickly became a standard possession for many, eventually most, American families. By the mid-Sixties more than 80 million motor vehicles crowded American highways; the number is expected to increase to well over 100 million within less than twenty years.

The consequences of this readily accepted change for American culture and society have been virtually incalculable. The automobile industry became one of the nation's greatest and a dominant component of the economy; the recession of 1958 was widely labeled an "automobile recession" because of a substantial dip in the industry's fortunes and its impact on the rest of the nation's business and economy. The automobile has played a major role in influencing the nature of urban and suburban growth. Leisure patterns have been changed; family life, religion, and politics influenced; birth rates and death rates affected. Few if any of these consequences were foreseen or expected; many were not desired. In gaining fame and fortune with his mass-produced Model T, Henry Ford helped to destroy the peaceful rural world he himself valued so highly.

The equilibrium of a social system, however, can be disrupted not only by cultural innovations, but also by dynamic processes generated by its own institutions. One of Karl Marx's chief contributions to the development of social science lay in his demonstration that accepted institutions could create the conditions that would eventually lead to their transformation. Conventional and approved capitalist

behavior, for example, has contributed to the transformation
of capitalism: Unrestricted competition in a free market
has steadily reduced the extent of competition in many
industries; the elimination of an employer's responsibilities
for his workers left them to the mercies of the market and
led to labor organization and the eventual reconstruction
of worker-employer relations. In some peasant societies, to
take an alternative illustration, inheritance rules calling
for equal division of land among sons may eventually create
such minuscule plots of land for farming that they will be
unable to support the families living upon them.

With changes continuously taking place in various
sectors of society, tensions, strains, and pressures for further
shifts are built up. Under some conditions, the readjustments necessary to resolve the difficulties which exist come
about relatively easily, through a democratic political process or by the efforts of those who recognize the need for
some changes. If groups of people are stimulated or pro-
voked by some difficulty for which there does not appear to
be a ready solution—if they cannot achieve their goals, or
their security or status is sharply challenged, or incompatible or excessive demands are made upon them—they
may deliberately seek to transform the existing state of
affairs by creating a *social movement*. Many of the changes
that do occur in society are at least in part the outcome
of more or less organized action on the part of such movements—for example, the prohibition movement, the Granger
movement, Naziism in Germany, the Mau Mau in Kenya,
the civil rights movement, the "Ban the Bomb" movement
in England of several years ago. Not all movements are
successful in achieving their goals; their efforts in fact often
lead to opposition movements that confront each other in
the political arena. Even if social movements do not ac-
complish their stated aims, they can nevertheless play an
important role in the shifting social order.

In the analysis of change, then, to summarize our discussion thus far, we must include influences from without, contact with other groups, institutionalized sources of change, the latent consequences of existing institutions and social structures, tensions generated by the lack of complete integration, and organized efforts to effect change. These are not unrelated forces, and their interrelations must be examined systematically in a sociological study.

Recognition of the complexity of social change and of the forces which initiate or provoke it should not lead to the conclusion that because a great many variables are involved "it does not make much difference which variable one starts with." [36] The equilibrium-interdependence approach that we have suggested undoubtedly leads, if systematically pursued, to the inclusion of almost the entire range of relevant variables. "In the end," as Kingsley Davis points out, "in order to explain the total change in a society, one would have to consider the main variables constituting the social equilibrium." [37] But specific changes can often be accounted for adequately without necessarily considering all aspects of the society. Even though a developed explanation of any change eventually encompasses a wide range of variables, it is necessary to assess the relative importance of each. In explaining the increasing professionalization of many occupations, for example, shifts in family organization or in religious beliefs seem to be much less significant than the development of new skills and the nature of the social and economic rewards available to those who successfully claim professional status.

Sociology and history

The analysis of specific types of social organization and of institutions and other cultural forms, we have suggested, must deal with problems of change as well as those of function and order. We wish to emphasize this concern with change because too much sociological work, particularly in the United States, has been directed to static studies, too little to problems of change. Any analysis, of course, necessarily emphasizes some facts and problems at the expense of others. Many sociological studies have merely sought to establish relationships among a given set of facts at a particular time and place—between size of organization and forms of authority, for example, or between class position and reading habits. Functional analysis has tended to emphasize problems of order and the maintenance of a given social system. But in a world of rapid and frequently revolutionary change, failure to give adequate attention to the shifts constantly taking place in the ways in which people live, in the ideas they live by, and in their relations with one another, must seriously limit the utility and applicability of sociological inquiry. As C. Wright Mills put it in a provocative and stimulating discussion of "The Uses of History," "Only by an act of abstraction that unnecessarily violates social reality can we try to freeze some knife-edge moment." [38]

We have chosen to call our approach to the study of social change "historical" for two reasons. First, we wish to emphasize the fact that all sociological inquiries refer to persons and actions at some specific time and place. Although sociologists try to derive propositions not limited by time or place, their analytic, ahistorical studies, whether of voting behavior, mental health, community power structure, class differences in behavior, or family disorganization, almost inevitably assume, implicitly, a given historical context. The greater the awareness of that context, the sources from which it is derived, and the tendencies toward change inherent in it, the greater the likelihood that more of the relevant variables will be taken into account and the less the possibility that generalizations derived from such studies will be extended to other circumstances where they do not apply.

Mills has argued that "There is . . . no 'law' stated by any social scientist that is trans-historical, that must not be understood as having to do with the specific structure of some period. Other 'laws' turn out to be empty abstractions or quite confused tautologies." [39] Mills seems to dismiss too cavalierly the possibility of generalizations that apply beyond specific historical situations, but he is correct in discounting many, perhaps most, of the "laws" that are now asserted to define universally found relationships among sociological variables. At best we can point at present to variables to be taken into account in dealing with particular problems and, at a very general level, to the conditions which must exist for certain events to take place or for various structures to survive. These are not unimportant contributions, but they remain still at some distance from general theory readily applicable to any and all societies. Some of our most useful sociological theories have, in fact, been explicitly confined to particular places and periods: theories of the American character and of the origins of modern capitalism, for example. Others, which were initially formulated in general terms—theories of the city, of bureaucracy, of industrial organization—have turned out to be far more historically confined than originally thought. Even if—or, perhaps more optimistically, when—adequate general sociological theory is available, the problem of its applicability to specific historical situations will still have to be resolved.

Second, we wish to stress the link between sociology and history. In so doing, however, it is necessary to distinguish between the two fields as well as to identify their affinities. These disciplines mean different things to the practitioners of each, and it is therefore difficult to draw clear lines and assign neatly demarcated fields of inquiry. There are many historians who might legitimately be identified as sociologists—and vice versa. Nevertheless, some rough distinctions can be drawn, for the historian's interests and focus of attention are, on the whole, different from those of the sociologist.

The historian is typically concerned with the past, but unless he is a pure antiquarian, he is also interested in its relevance to the present. The sociologist, on the other hand, is much more likely to focus his attention upon the present, although there are some—and there should be more—exceptions to this self-imposed limitation.

Many historians disclaim any identification as scientists; their aim is narrative, to describe *wie es eigentlich gewesen ist* (as it really was), in the oft-quoted phrase of the great German historian Ranke. They are "scientific" only insofar as they seek the most reliable data. Much of the narrative deals with concrete persons and presumably unique events. The sociologist, on the other hand, as we noted earlier, is centrally concerned with generalizations. Individuals and events are important chiefly as they fit into categories or patterns. Abstraction, inevitable in any intellectual discourse (including history), is explicit, self-conscious, and typically at a higher level than in historical scholarship.

The English economic historian Michael Postan has argued, however, that the "uniqueness" and the "concreteness" of historical study are essentially "fictitious," for if historical investigations were truly unique and concrete, actually limited to specific persons and events, they would be dull and uninteresting. Only when comparisons or generalizations are suggested or implied does historical study become truly valuable. Nevertheless, he asserts, the historian must maintain these fictions, else he will lose his distinctive identity and fail to make his distinctive contribution. Despite—or perhaps because of—this mild and, if Postan is right, fruitful self-deception, the creative historian does have something to contribute to the effort to create a "science of society." [40]

In addition, a good deal of historical inquiry actually

deals not with individual persons and unique events, but with institutions, organizations, beliefs, and ideas—that is, with social structure and culture. In these areas the historian obviously deals with materials and problems similar to those of the sociologist. The differences lie in the extent to which explicit general concepts are used, in the emphasis upon the concrete and unique in one case and on the general and recurrent in the other, and in a greater concern with change on the part of the historian. Each, therefore, has something to contribute to the other, although at present it appears that more historians are benefiting from their exposure to sociology than the other way around.

Conclusion

The contrast between the functional and historical approaches is itself in all likelihood merely a phase in the history of sociology. If this now barely maturing discipline is to achieve its goals and fulfill its youthful hopes, these approaches—and the theories they have engendered—must be brought together into a unified whole. Already they share several common perspectives. They both entail an awareness of the complex interrelationships which exist within society and of the limitations of any simplified one-factor interpretation of social behavior. They are both concerned with generalization rather than with the individual and unique, and they utilize similar concepts for catching the recurrent aspects of social life. Finally, they both recognize the importance and value of a comparative approach, for whatever the problems selected for study the systematic comparison of different societies, past and present, provides both the basis for suggestive hypotheses and the material for testing them.

Notes

[1] Ralph Ross, *Symbols and Civilization* (New York: Harcourt, 1962), p. 64.

[2] For a full analysis of the "modes of the question 'Why?'" see Robert M. MacIver, *Social Causation* (Boston: Ginn, 1942), especially Part III.

[3] See, for example, the articles by Talcott Parsons, Robert N. Bellah, and S. N. Eisenstadt, *American Sociological Review,* XXIX (June, 1964).

[4] For an essay that argues that sociological analysis *is* functional analysis, see Kingsley Davis, "The Myth of Functional Analysis," *American Sociological Review,* XXIV (December, 1959), 757–72.

[5] Robert K. Merton, *Social Theory and Social Structure* (rev. and enlarged ed.; New York: Free Press, 1957), p. 46. Much of the following discussion of functional analysis is derived from Ch. 1.

[6] Gerhart Niemeyer, *Law Without Force* (Princeton: Princeton University Press, 1941), p. 300, quoted in Merton, *op. cit.,* p. 46 *n.*

[7] Quoted in Lewis A. Coser and Bernard Rosenberg (eds.), *Sociological Theory* (2nd ed.; New York: Macmillan, 1964), p. 622.

[8] Émile Durkheim, *The Rules of Sociological Method,* trans. by Sarah A. Solovay and John H. Mueller, ed. with an intro. by George E. G. Catlin (Chicago: University of Chicago Press, 1938), p. 95.

[9] See David Aberle *et al.,* "The Functional Prerequisites of a Society," *Ethics* IX (January, 1950), 100–11, for an effort to spell out a minimum set of functional prerequisites (or, more precisely, requisites).

[10] For a useful analysis of the risks of a functional analysis of religion, see Merton, *op. cit.,* pp. 28–30.

[11] William F. Cottrell, "Of Time and the Railroader," *American Sociological Review,* IV (April, 1939), 190–8.

[12] Merton, *op. cit.,* p. 51.

[13] Quoted in Louis Schneider, "Problems in the Sociology of Religion," in Robert E. L. Faris (ed.), *Handbook of Modern Sociology* (Chicago: Rand McNally, 1964), p. 783.

[14] *Ibid.*, p. 784.

[15] Charles A. Beard and Mary R. Beard, *The Rise of American Civilization*, II (New York: Macmillan, 1930), p. 778.

[16] Liston Pope, *Millhands and Preachers* (New Haven: Yale University Press, 1942), pp. 84–91 and Ch. VIII.

[17] For a suggestive exposition of the latent functions of the political machine, see Merton, *op. cit.*, pp. 72–82. For an attempt to place Merton's analysis in a historical context, see Eric L. McKitrick, "The Study of Corruption," *Political Science Quarterly*, LXXII (December, 1957), 502–14.

[18] Marion J. Levy, *The Structure of Society* (Princeton: Princeton University Press, 1952), pp. 76–83.

[19] Max Gluckman, *Custom and Conflict in Africa* (Oxford: Blackwell, 1955), p. 111.

[20] *Ibid.*, pp. 113–4.

[21] *Ibid.*, p. 115.

[22] *Ibid.*, pp. 115–6.

[23] *The New York Times,* April 19, 1959.

[24] Barrington Moore, Jr., *Terror and Progress: U.S.S.R.* (Cambridge, Mass.: Harvard University Press, 1954), p. 62.

[25] Zena S. Blau, "Exposure to Child-Rearing Experts: A Structural Interpretation of Class-Color Differences," *American Journal of Sociology*, LXIX (May, 1964), 596–608.

[26] Melvin L. Kohn, "Social Class and Parent-Child Relationships: An Interpretation," *American Journal of Sociology*, LXVIII (January, 1963), 471–80.

[27] Robert M. MacIver and Charles H. Page, *Society: An Introductory Analysis* (New York: Holt, 1949), p. 589.

[28] Julian H. Steward, "Evolution and Progress," in Alfred L. Kroeber *et al., Anthropology Today* (Chicago: University of Chicago Press, 1953), p. 315.

[29] W. Lloyd Warner, *A Black Civilization* (New York: Harper, 1937).

[30] Talcott Parsons, "Evolutionary Universals in Society," *American Sociological Review,* XXIX (June, 1964), 339–57. See also Parsons, *Societies: Evolutionary and Comparative Perspectives* (Englewood Cliffs: Prentice-Hall, 1966).

[31] Wilbert E. Moore, *Social Change* (Englewood Cliffs: Prentice-Hall, 1963), p. 116.

[32] C. Wright Mills, *The Sociological Imagination* (New York: Oxford, 1959), p. 150.

[33] Ralph Linton, *The Study of Man* (New York: Appleton, 1936), pp. 326–7.

[34] Ralf Dahrendorf, "Out of Utopia: Toward a Reorientation of Sociological Analysis," *American Journal of Sociology,* LXIV (September, 1958), 115–27.

[35] Lewis A. Coser, *The Functions of Social Conflict* (New York: Free Press, 1956).

[36] Kingsley Davis, *Human Society* (New York: Macmillan, 1949), p. 634.

[37] *Ibid.*

[38] Mills, *op. cit.,* p. 151.

[39] *Ibid.,* pp. 149–50.

[40] Michael M. Postan, "History and the Social Sciences," in *The Social Sciences: Their Relations in Theory and in Teaching* (London: LePlay, 1936), pp. 60–70.

Suggestions for further reading

BIERSTEDT, ROBERT. "Toynbee and Sociology," *British Journal of Sociology,* X (June, 1959), 95–104.
A brief summary of the differences and interrelationships between sociology and history.

DURKHEIM, ÉMILE. *The Rules of Sociological Method.* Trans. by Sarah A. Solovay and John H. Mueller. Edited with an intro-

duction by George E. G. Catlin. 8th ed. Chicago: University of Chicago Press, 1938, Ch. 5, "Rules for the Explanation of Social Facts."
The classic formulation of the difference between functional and causal (historical) analysis.

KOMAROVSKY, MIRRA (ED.). *Common Frontiers of the Social Sciences*. New York: Free Press, 1957, Part I, "History and Social Research."
A series of essays, theoretical and substantive, dealing with and illustrating the relations between historical analysis and sociological research.

LINTON, RALPH. *The Study of Man*. New York: Appleton, 1936, Chs. 18, "Discovery and Invention," and 19, "Diffusion."
Brief but useful discussions of innovation and diffusion based upon anthropological research.

MACIVER, ROBERT M., AND CHARLES H. PAGE. *Society: An Introductory Analysis*. New York: Holt, 1949, Book III, "Social Change."
A critical review of alternative theories of social change, a reinterpretation of the nature of social evolution, and a brief summary of some long-run trends in the development of modern society.

MERTON, ROBERT K. *Social Theory and Social Structure*. Revised and enlarged ed. New York: Free Press, 1957, Ch. 1, "Manifest and Latent Functions."
A comprehensive and critical discussion of the concept of function, including a paradigm for functional analysis that seeks to avoid many of the pitfalls it contains.

MILLS, C. WRIGHT. *The Sociological Imagination*. New York: Oxford, 1959, Ch. 8, "Uses of History."
An excellent discussion of the relevance of history for sociological analysis.

MOORE, WILBERT E. *Social Change*. Englewood Cliffs: Prentice-Hall, 1963.
A very useful short book that attempts to formulate an approach to and interpretation of problems of social change.

index

ABEGGLEN, JAMES, 140, 154n.

ABERLE, DAVID, 196n.

abstraction in sociology, 21, 24, 25, 40, 120–1, 122, 194

achievement: and class, 78; and status, 67–8

ADORNO, THEODORE, 147, 154n., 155n.

age-grading, 96

agriculture, 114

alcoholism and ethnic groups, 122

ALEXANDER, FRANZ, 154n.

Alor, child-rearing in, 146–7

Andaman Islands, society of, 45, 91

ANSHEN, RUTH N., 116n.

AQUINAS, THOMAS, 7

ARCHER, WILLIAM, 87n.

ARISTOTLE, 12, 40–1, 63, 101, 116n., 144–5, 155n.

ASCH, SOLOMON, 28, 37n.

ascription: and class, 78; and ethnic-group membership, 77; and status, 67–8

associational society, 81, 83–6

associations: and primary groups, 78–9; as secondary groups, 76

AUSTEN, JANE, 5

"authoritarian personality," 140–1, 147–8

authority, 182; and socialization, 140–1

baby-care manuals, 175–7

BACON, FRANCIS, 8, 20

BALDWIN, JAMES M., 136

BALTZELL, E. DIGBY, 153n.

BARRON, MILTON L., 35n.

BEARD, CHARLES A., 197n.

BEARD, MARY R., 197n.

BECKER, HOWARD, 81

Belgium, ethnic divisions in, 164

beliefs as ideas, 56–8

BELLAH, ROBERT N., 196n.

BENEDICT, RUTH, 128, 150, 154n., 155n.

BETTELHEIM, BRUNO, 86n.

BIERSTEDT, ROBERT, 36n., 37n.

biology: and family, 76; and individual differences, 149–50; and race, 101–7; and role, 66; and society, 97–107

birth rates, 32, 97

BLAU, ZENA, 177, 197n.

BOROFF, DAVID, 88n.

brainwashing, 143–4

BRIM, ORVILLE G., JR., 155

BROOM, LEONARD, 36n., 155n.

BRYSON, GLADYS, 42, 87n.

bureaucracy, 97; in associational societies, 84; as concept, 24–5; as recurring form, 96; and secondary groups, 76

BURGESS, JOHN W., 115n.

CALVIN, JOHN, 7

capitalism, 9, 189–90, 193

CASSIRER, ERNST, 58, 87n.

Catholics, U.S., 168; *see also* Roman Catholic Church

CATLIN, GEORGE E. G., 196n.

CENTERS, RICHARD, 153n., 154n.

CHAMBERLAIN, HOUSTON STEWART, 102

character, 66

CHILD, IRVIN L., 155

child-rearing: cultural definitions of, 144; and love, 124–5; manuals for, 175–7; and socialization, 130–4, 137–41, 142, 143, 150–1; and social structure, 147; *see also* family

CHINOY, ELY, 88n., 155n.

CHINOY, HELEN KRICH, 87n.

CHURCH, JOSEPH, 153n.

cities, 80

class, 24, 45; and ethnic differences, 77–8; and personality, 124, 126–8; and socialization, 134, 143, 147, 150

class consciousness, 73, 78, 92; of manual workers, 128–9

climate and culture, 110–4

clines, 104

CLOWARD, RICHARD A., 36n.

COHEN, ALBERT K., 36n.

COHEN, MORRIS R., 21, 36n.

COLE, TOBY, 87n.

Comanche Indians, 91

"common sense" and science, 10, 15–6, 33–4

communal society, 81–3, 85–6

communication as social process, 58, 100

Communism as religion, 98–9

communities, 24; as social group, 80

COMTE, AUGUSTE, 3, 159, 160, 178

concepts: and jargon, 14–8; nature of, 18–22; uses of, 22–6

conflict in society, 187

"conflict model" versus equilibrium model, 187

conformity: and institutions, 51–2, 54–5, 56, 165; "modes of," 147; and socialization, 129, 130, 134, 143, 147–8

consensus, 85, 187

contract as societal base, 81

COOLEY, CHARLES HORTON, 39–40, 86n., 136, 137, 138, 154n.

COON, CARLETON S., 116n.

COQUELIN, CONSTANT, 87n.

COSER, LEWIS, 187, 196n., 198n.

COTTRELL, LEONARD S., JR., 36n., 155n.

COTTRELL, WILLIAM F., 196n.

crime, 55, 111

cultural absolutism, 93–4

cultural relativity, 93–4

culture, 26; and climate, 110–4; components of, 49–58; definition of, 45–9; and diffusion, 182–5; Freudian view of, 148–9; and geography, 110–4; as ideational, 46, 56–8; and individual, 119–52; and language, 58, 100; material, 59–60; organization of, 60–1; and sex differences, 107–10; and social character, 144–9; and society, 39–86; variation and diversity of, 90–115 custom, 51; versus laws, 52–3

DAHRENDORF, RALF, 198*n*.
DAVIS, KINGSLEY, 86*n*., 87*n*., 191, 196*n*., 198*n*.
delinquency, 55
delinquent gangs, 24, 31
DEMOCRITUS, 63
DENNY, REUEL, 155*n*.
determinism: biological, 97–110; geographical, 110–4; and social change, 181–2
deviant behavior, 24, 25, 55
diffusion, 182–5
discrimination and ethnic groups, 79
diversity in society, 90–115
division of labor, 83
divorce, 55
DOLLARD, JOHN, 27, 37*n*.
DOSTOYEVSKY, FEODOR, 5
drives: channeling of, 134, 149; and cultural diversity, 99–101; Freudian view of, 138
DU BOIS, CORA, 155*n*.
DURKHEIM, ÉMILE, 19, 36*n*., 81, 114, 117*n*., 160, 196*n*.
dynamics: concept of, 159–60; and function, 180–1
dysfunction, definition of, 170–1

ecology, 25
economic determinism, 181
economic growth, 174–5, 181–2
education as socializing agency, 131–3, 141, 142, 143
Ego-ideal, 139
EISENSTADT, S. N., 196*n*.
ELLIS, WILLIAM, 116*n*., 155*n*.
empiricism and science, 7, 8
endogenous change, 182; and equilibrium, 186–91
England, 141; colonialism of, 185
equalitarianism, 78
equilibrium and social change, 186–91

Eskimos, 81, 91, 113
ethnic groups, 24, 45, 78; and associations, 79; and class, 77, 79; definition of, 76–7; and discrimination, 79; and family, 77; and the individual, 122, 125–6
ethnocentrism, 9, 47, 94
eufunction, 9, 47, 94
evolutionary theory in sociology, 178–80
exogenous change, diffusion as, 182–5

family: in associational society, 83, 84; biological bases of, 76, 98; in communal society, 81–2; and ethnic groups, 77; Freudian view of, 138; functions of, 163; nuclear, 176; and personality, 136–41; as primary group, 75–6; as socializing agency, 129–30, 137–41, 163; in the United States 175–7, 189; universality of, 95
FARIS, ROBERT E. L., 197*n*.
feminine roles, 107–10, 146
feral man, 41, 119
FERENCZI, SANDOR, 153*n*.
FERGUSON, ADAM, 41, 63, 86*n*.
FIRTH, RAYMOND, 116*n*.
folk society, 81
folkways, 51–2
FREDERICK II, EMPEROR, 123–4
FRENKEL-BRUNSWIK, ELSE, 147
FREUD, SIGMUND, 138–9, 143, 148, 154*n*.
FRIEDAN, BETTY, 109–10, 116*n*.
FROMM, ERICH, 109, 116*n*.
function: as concept, 161–3; latent and manifest, 167–71
functional alternatives in society, 165
functional analysis in sociology, 161–77, 179–81, 192, 195
functionalism: definition of, 160; versus historical approach, 159–61

GALBRAITH, JOHN K., 57, 87n.
gambling, latent function of, 169
Gemeinschaft, 81
geography and culture, 110–4
Gesellschaft, 81
GIBBON, EDWARD, 168
GIDDINGS, FRANKLIN H., 71
GINSBERG, MORRIS, 72, 79, 88n.
GLAZER, NATHAN, 155n.
GLUCKMAN, MAX, 171–2, 197n.
GOBINEAU, ARTHUR DE, 102
GOULDNER, ALVIN W., 88n.
GROSS, LLEWELLYN, 36n.
group marriage, 98
groups, 24, 50, 51–2; characteris-
    tics of, 68–74; peer, 130, 143;
    secondary, 76; types of, 74–80;
    see also associations; ethnic
    groups; primary groups

HALL, CALVIN, 154n.
HARTLEY, EUGENE, 37n.
heredity and society, 101–2
HERODOTUS, 68
Hindus, 91, 105
historical analysis, 159; and so-
    cial change, 177–82
historical approach versus func-
    tionalism, 159–61
history and sociology, 191–5
HITLER, ADOLF, 104
HOBBES, THOMAS, 119
HOEBEL, E. ADAMSON, 153n.
HUNT, EDWARD E., JR., 116n.

ideas as component of culture,
    56–8
identification, 138–9, 140
incest taboo, 92–3, 96, 97
India, ascription in, 78
individuality: culture and, 119–
    52; as differentiation, 149–51;
    and socialization, 129–44; as
    social product, 123–6; society
    and, 119–52; sociological expla-
    nation of, 126–9

industrialization, 173–5; and in-
    vention, 188–9
industrial society, 81
INKELES, ALEX, 155n.
innovation, technological, 188–9
insects, social, 100
instincts and cultural diversity,
    100
institutions, 24; as component of
    culture, 49–56; crescive, 54; defi-
    nition of, 49–50; economic,
    95–6; enacted, 52–3; and func-
    tional analysis, 165, 166, 168–
    70; as normative patterns, 49–
    56, 130; and social change, 177,
    179, 182, 186–91; and social
    character, 144, 146–9; and so-
    cialization, 130–3, 143, 186
internalization and personality,
    137, 138–9
invention and social change,
    188–9
Israel, socialization in, 130

JACQUES, ELLIOTT, 154n.
JAMES, WILLIAM, 136
Japan, Westernization of, 185
jargon, problem of, 14–8
Jews: and alcoholism, 122; and
    pain, 125–6; and racial the-
    ory, 102, 106
JOHNSON, SAMUEL, 5

KARDINER, ABRAM, 154n., 155n.
KELLER, HELEN, 58
KILLIAN, LEWIS M., 37n.
kinship system, 129, 130, 165, 179;
    see also family
KIRK, RUSSELL, 35n.
KLUCKHOHN, CLYDE, 86n., 101,
    115n., 154n.
KOHN, MELVIN L., 197n.
KOMAROVSKY, MIRRA, 87n.
KROEBER, ALFRED L., 11, 36n., 86n.,
    87n., 115n., 116n., 197n.

language: and self, 136; and social class, 126–7; symbolic, 58
latent function, 167–71
law, 51, 52–3; in associational versus communal societies, 82–3
LAZARSFELD, PAUL F., 36*n*.
leisure, 84, 189
LEVINSON, DANIEL J., 147
LEVY, MARION, 170, 197*n*.
LINDZEY, GARDNER, 154*n*.
LINNAEUS, CAROLUS, 102
LINTON, RALPH, 44, 46–7, 87*n*., 115*n*., 123, 149, 153*n*., 155*n*., 183–4, 198*n*.
LOMBARD, GEORGE F. F., 153*n*.
LYND, HELEN M., 95, 115*n*.
LYND, ROBERT S., 95, 115*n*.

MACCOBY, ELEANOR E., 37*n*.
MACHIAVELLI, NICCOLÒ, 5
MACIVER, ROBERT M., 12, 36*n*., 57, 87*n*., 155*n*., 178, 196*n*., 197*n*.
MCKITRICK, ERIC L., 197*n*.
MCLAUGHLIN, MARY M., 153*n*.
MAIER, JOSEPH, 87*n*.
MAINE, HENRY, 81
MALINOWSKI, BRONISLAW, 154*n*.
MANDELBAUM, DAVID, 153*n*.
MANDEVILLE, BERNARD DE, 12, 36*n*.
manifest function, 167–71
MANNHEIM, KARL, 37*n*.
MARETT, R. R., 87*n*.
marriage: monogamous, 96, 98; polygynous, 98; *see also* family
MARX, KARL, 181, 189
masculinity, definitions of, 107–9, 142, 146
mass media as socializing agency, 131–2, 133, 135, 143, 151
mass persuasion, 147–8
material culture, 59–60
MAYO, ELTON, 153*n*.
MEAD, GEORGE HERBERT, 136–7, 138, 139, 154*n*.
MEAD, MARGARET, 116*n*., 154*n*.
mechanical solidarity, 81

MERTON, ROBERT K., 10, 35*n*., 36*n*., 37*n*., 155*n*., 161, 169, 196*n*., 197*n*.
middle class: child-rearing in, 124, 134, 143, 176–7; diction of, 126–7; socialization in, 147, 150
militant society, 81
MILLER, WRIGHT, 155*n*.
MILLS, C. WRIGHT, 35, 37*n*., 182, 192, 193, 198*n*.
MITFORD, NANCY, 153*n*.
models, behavior, 135, 139
MOLIÈRE (JEAN BAPTISTE POQUELIN), 18
monogamy, 96, 98
MONTAGU, M. F. ASHLEY, 86*n*.
MONTAIGNE, MICHEL EYQUEM DE, 5
MONTESQUIEU, CHARLES LOUIS DE, 5, 110–1, 116*n*.
MOORE, BARRINGTON, JR., 197*n*.
MOORE, WILBERT E., 180, 198*n*.
mores, 51–2, 53, 61; in associational societies, 84–5; in communal societies, 82–3; and cultural diversity, 91–2
MORRIS, WILLIAM, 59
Moslems, 91
MUELLER, JOHN H., 196*n*.
MURDOCK, GEORGE, 46, 94, 115*n*.
MURRAY, HENRY A., 154*n*.

NAGEL, ERNEST, 21, 36*n*.
national character, 144–6
Negroes, 11, 13, 72; attitudes toward, 27–30, 142; class position of, 79; and racial theory, 102, 103–4, 106; as statistical aggregate, 73
NEWCOMB, THEODORE, 37*n*.
NIEMEYER, GERHART, 196*n*.
nonconformity, 55; and socialization, 134, 143
normative patterns, institutions as, 49–56, 130
norms, *see* social norms

objectivity in science, 8–14
OGBURN, WILLIAM F., 86*n*.

OHLIN, LLOYD E., 36n.
organic solidarity, 81
organizations, formal, 76

PAGE, CHARLES H., 37n., 87n., 155n., 178, 197n.
parent, "introjected" (or internalized), 138–9
PARSONS, TALCOTT, 25, 35n., 36n., 66, 87n., 88n., 179, 196n., 198n.
pattern variables, 25
peer groups and socialization, 130, 131, 132, 143
personality: components of, 135–41; psychological versus sociological perspectives of, 119–23; and role, 66; and society, 119–52; use of as term, 135
PIAGET, JEAN, 137–8, 154n.
PLATO, 5
political corruption, latent function of, 169
political discontent, 171
polyandry, 98
polygyny, 98
Polynesians, 91
POPE, LISTON, 168, 197n.
POSTAN, MICHAEL, 194, 198n.
power, 164–5, 170, 182
primary groups: definition of, 75, 78–9; and the individual, 136
primitive society: and cultural relativism, 93–4; limits, as defined in, 164; and social function, 167; socialization in, 96
professionalization, 191
psychoanalysis, 138–9, 140
psychology, perspective of, 119–23

Quakers, 128
quasi-groups, 72

race and society, 101–7, 146; *see also* ethnic groups; Negroes
racism, 73, 102–3

RANKE, LEOPOLD VON, 194
rationality in science, 7
REDFIELD, ROBERT, 81, 83, 88n.
religion, 168, 189, 191; universality of, 98–9
repression and culture, 148–9
RETZIUS, GUSTAV, 116n.
RIESMAN, DAVID, 147, 155n.
ritual: diversity of, 98; functional analysis of, 167, 169, 171–3
roles, 24; in associational societies, 83; and biology, 66; in communal societies, 81–3; inclusive, 82, 83; occupational, 142; and personality, 66; segmental, 76, 82, 83; and social change, 177; and socialization, 130, 132, 141–3, 151; and status, 61–8
Roman Catholic Church, 69–70, 96
ROSENBERG, BERNARD, 196n.
ROSS, JAMES B., 153n.
ROSS, RALPH, 7, 36n., 196n.
ROUSSEAU, JEAN JACQUES, 119
RUMNEY, JAY, 87n.

sacred society, 81
SAINT-SIMON, HENRI DE, 178
sanctions, 56; and conformity, 130, 144
SANFORD, R. NEVITT, 147
SAPIR, EDWARD, 121
SCHNEIDER, DAVID M., 154n.
SCHNEIDER, LOUIS, 197n.
science: concepts of, 14–26; nature of, 3–7, 63; objectivity of, 8–14; and sociology, 3–35, 159; and theory, 27–33; values of, 8–14
secondary groups, 76
secular society, 81
self and society, 135–40, 150
self-image, 135, 136
sex differences and society, 100, 107–10
sex mores, 55; and cultural relativism, 92–4
sex roles, 64, 65; biological basis of, 107–10; and child-rearing,

sex roles (*continued*)
176; definitions of, 66, 107–10, 142, 146
sex taboos, 92–3, 96, 97
sexual gratification, 125, 148; as family function, 163
SHAKESPEARE, WILLIAM, 5, 62, 63
SHAPIRO, HARRY L., 153n.
SHAW, GEORGE BERNARD, 72
SHILS, EDWARD, 35n.
SIMMEL, GEORG, 44, 87n.
social category: definition of, 71; and groups, 72–3, 77–8
social change, 160; in associational societies, 84–5; and child-rearing, 132–3; and diffusion, 182–5; and equilibrium, 186–91; exogenous versus endogenous, 182; and historical approach, 177–82; and individual versus society, 149; and movements, 190; and technology, 188–9; theories of, 178–81
social character and social structure, 144–9
social class, *see* class
social function, 160
social groups, *see* groups
"social heritage," 49
socialization, 56; adult, 141–4; agencies of, 129–33; anticipatory, 142; and child-rearing, 130–4, 137–41, 142, 143, 150–1; and family, 129–30, 137–41, 163; and individual differences, 149–51; process of, 133–41; and social structure, 144–9
social mobility, 169
social movements and change, 190
social norms: and cultural diversity, 90–115; and individual, 120; and institutions, 50, 52–3, 54, 56; and social change, 177; and socialization, 119–52; in social structure, 160; *see also* values
social organization, 50, 95, 96; and biology, 97–107; forms of, 68–86

social relationships, 24; in associational societies, 83–4; in communal societies, 82–3; concept of, 43–4; and culture, 58; and roles, 66, 81–4
social structure: definition of, 69; and functional analysis, 179–81; and social change, 182; and social character, 144–9
social values, *see* values
society: associational, 81, 83–6; bases of, 81; and biology, 97–107; communal, 81–3, 85–6; and community, 80; conflict in, 187; and culture, 39–86; defined, 42–5; diffusion in, 182–5; diversity in, 90–115; equilibrium versus change in, 186–91; and individual, 119–52; industrial, 81; militant, 81; power in, 164–5; and race, 101–7; types of, 81–6; uniformity in, 90–115
sociological explanation, 126–9
sociology: analytical modes of, 158–95; concepts of, 14–26; evolutionary theory in, 178–80; functional analysis in, 161–77, 179–81, 192, 195; historical analysis in, 159, 177–82, 191–5; and individual, 119–29; and jargon, 14–8; "laws" of, 193; versus psychological perspectives, 119–23; and science, 3–35, 159; sources of, 3–7; and theory, 27–33; value of, 33–5
solidarity, 81
SOLOVAY, SARAH A., 196n.
Soviet Union, 77, 96–7; industrialization of, 112; religion in, 98–9; *tolkachi* in, 173–5
SPENCER, HERBERT, 34, 36n., 37n., 49, 81, 178
SPITZ, RENÉ A., 124, 153n.
SPOCK, BENJAMIN, 175, 177
SPROTT, W. J. H., 154n.
statistical aggregates, 71–4
status: achieved and ascribed, 67–8, 78; and biology, 66; and

status (*continued*)
  personality, 121; and role, 61–8;
  seeking of, 68; as societal base,
  81
STEWARD, JULIAN, 178, 197n.
STONE, L. JOSEPH, 153n.
STOUFFER, SAMUEL A., 115n.
subcultures, 165
success ideology, 148, 169–70
suicide, 55, 111, 159
SUMNER, WILLIAM GRAHAM, 50, 51,
  54, 87n., 92
superego, 138–9

taboos: and functional analysis,
  171–3; incest, 93–3, 96, 97
TAYLOR, GRIFFITH, 116n.
technology, 181, 185; and innovation, 188–9
theory, nature of, 27–33
tolkach, 173–5
TOLSTOY, LEO, 145, 155n.
TÖNNIES, FERDINAND, 81
totalitarian societies, 13, 104, 152,
  170; mass media in, 131–2
tradition: and associational society, 84–5; and law, 82–3
Trobriand Islanders, 60, 134
TYLOR, EDWARD, 41, 46

uniformity in society, 90–115
unilineal social evolution, 178
United States: 78, 91–3, 96–7, 112,
  127; family in, 175–7; innova-

United States (*continued*)
  tion in, 188–9; and race, 102–4;
  socialization in, 131, 141, 150;
  success ideology in, 148, 169–
  70
urban society, 81, 83

values, 57–8; and groups, 126–7;
  of science, 8–14; and social
  change, 84–5; and socialization,
  134–5, 147
VEBLEN, THORSTEIN, 181

WARD, LESTER F., 178
WARNER, W. LLOYD, 140, 154n.,
  198n.
WATERMAN, THOMAS T., 116n.
WHEELER, STANTON, 155n.
WHITEHEAD, ALFRED N., 6, 35n.
WHITING, JOHN W. M., 155n.
WILLIAMS, RAYMOND, 87n.
WILLIAMS, ROBIN M., JR., 88n.
WILLMOTT, PETER, 88n.
WISSLER, CLARK, 95, 115n.
women, family role of, 176–7
working class: child-rearing in,
  176–7; class-consciousness of,
  127–8

YOUNG, MICHAEL, 88n.

ZBOROWSKI, MARK, 125, 153n.